KINGDOM PRINCIPLES

FOR
CHURCH GROWTH

Gene Mims

Revised and Expanded

LifeWay Press®
Nashville, Tennessee

Revised Edition © Copyright 2001 • LifeWay Press®
Original Edition © Copyright 1994 • Convention Press
Ninth Printing • November 2006

ISBN 0-7673-1889-7

This book is a text for course number LS-0054 and LS-0055 in the subject area
Sunday School, LS-0067 in the subject are Associational Office Management, LS-
0068 in the subject area Pastoral Ministries, LS-0082 in the subject area Church
Media Program, LS-0097 in the subject area Deacons, LS-0180 in the subject area
Church Secretaries, and LS-0186 in the subject area Vocational Preparation of the
Christian Growth Study Plan.

Dewey Decimal Classification: 254.5
Subject Headings: Church Growth/Evangelistic Work

To order additional copies of this resource: write LifeWay Church Resources
Customer Service; One LifeWay Plaza; Nashville, TN 37234-0113; fax order to
(615) 251-5933; phone toll free (800) 458-2772; e-mail at orderentry@lifeway.com;
order online at www.lifeway.com; or visit the LifeWay Christian Store serving you.

Printed in the United States of America

LifeWay Church Resources, a division of
LifeWay Christian Resources
of the Southern Baptist Convention
One LifeWay Plaza
Nashville, TN 37234-0175

TABLE OF CONTENTS

Foreword

Kingdom Principles for Church Growth has truly been a surprise and a joy. The surprise is that it has now been used around the world by ordinary people in the kingdom of God for extraordinary results. Mega-churches, small churches, and churches of various denominations have used it for their own purposes. Wow! What a tremendous surprise and blessing for me.

It is a joy because this second edition is a labor involving many people at LifeWay Christian Resources. The men and women I serve with at this wonderful place have made this a resource for many more persons than I could have ever imagined. I want to thank Mike Miller, Henry Webb, and Mark Marshall for their encouragement and support. And a special thanks to Norma Goldman for her tireless effort to complete this on time and in great shape!

As with the first edition, I dedicate this book
to my wife Ann, my loving companion and fellow servant of the Lord,
and
to our children, Jeff and Marianne,
who delight us with their lives each day.

INTRODUCTION

CHURCH LEADER'S PRAYER

Dear Lord, Sunday was a hard day at church. Things did not go well. Our church is not growing, and I'm so empty. I should know what You want me and my church to do to be a part of Your kingdom's work, but I don't have a clue.

What can I do to help my church grow? So much of my time is taken up by phone calls, wrestling with problems, and a thousand other job demands.

Lord, I hear about so many church growth plans. New methods! Old methods! Contemporary approaches! Traditional approaches! Which one do I try next? I'm so confused. What do *You* want me and my church to do?

If I don't know how to grow a church, how can I expect those I lead to know? My heart sinks when members ask, What are we going to try this year? What can I tell them?

MOVING TOWARD THE ANSWER

I have sat where you sit. My heart also sinks when I hear pastors, staff, and laypersons talk about their dismay and discouragement. Who of us has not felt these frustrations? These feelings are more prevalent than we like to admit.

What is happening to us and our churches? In our pursuit of the latest church growth methods, have we lost our understanding of God's plan for His church and our commitment to be part of His plan? Church growth methods are important, but they never can take the place of following the clear commands of our Lord.

We can become so wrapped up in trying one new method of church growth after another that we lose our God-given directions. We can depart from God's essential principles and lose sight of His kingdom and our part in it.

5

ESSENTIAL PRINCIPLES

This book is about God's kingdom principles of church growth. It is a return to biblical principles. It begins where God begins. It retraces our steps to rediscover, or perhaps discover for the first time, God's church growth process.

Church growth is born and nourished through a process given by God Himself. This book outlines that divinely inspired process rather than a church growth method.

To help you clearly and thoroughly understand the principles of this process, the concept of the *1·5·4 Principle* is introduced in these pages. The *1·5·4 Principle* involves:

> *1* driving force of church growth:
> The Great Commission
>
> *5* essential church functions for church growth:
> Evangelism
> Discipleship
> Fellowship
> Ministry
> Worship
>
> *4* results:
> Numerical Growth
> Spiritual Transformation
> Ministry Expansion
> Kingdom Advance

Church growth begins with kingdom principles, not with methods.

PROCESS VS. METHODS

One of the greatest dangers we face today in church growth is making methods supreme. Methods used in the fastest growing church in your area may not work in your church, but God's principles of church growth will work in every church. Before we can implement methods, we must understand the process God uses to redeem the world through the witness of the church.

Church growth is a leading topic today. It should be. The population of the world is growing every second

One of the greatest dangers we face is making methods supreme in church growth.

while some churches and denominations are plateauing or declining at an alarming rate. Still, we must not become so preoccupied with the search for the right method to reach an exploding population of lost people that we forget that an understanding of God's principles for kingdom growth is primary.

GROWTH BEGINS WITH DIVINE PROCESS

Methods of church growth are important, but God does not begin with methods. He begins with a divine process, and we must begin where He begins.

Somehow in our rush to find methods, we have forgotten that the kingdom of God, announced by Christ at the beginning of His ministry (Mark 1:14-15), is a reality in our world. That kingdom is energized by God Himself. The Bible frequently refers to God's kingdom as the outworking of His plan of world redemption.

Scripture reveals God consistently doing two things: creating and redeeming. He chose to create humanity in His image to have fellowship with Him and with one another. God chose to create every person with a will by which he or she accepts or rejects Him.

Scripture shows Adam and Eve turning away from God in disobedience and losing the opportunity to fellowship with Him. The story of humanity is the story of every person turning away from God in sin because every person is a sinner by nature and by choice.

GOD CHOSE TO REDEEM

In spite of our sin, God chose to redeem a people for Himself out of the world. Redemption restores the benefits lost in the fall and provides the redeemed with fellowship with God and one another.

When Jesus came to earth, He brought salvation to persons who were in sin and separated from God. He came preaching the good news of the kingdom and urging people to repent of their sins and to trust in Him.

"'The time is fulfilled, and the kingdom of God has come near. Repent and believe in the good news!'... 'Follow Me,' Jesus told them, 'and I will make you into fishers of men!'" (Mark 1:15,17).

> Kingdom process, revealed and energized by God Himself, is where we must begin.

> Jesus proclaimed the coming of the kingdom.

THE KINGDOM CONTINUES TO GROW

The Bible declares that the kingdom of God is growing and cannot be stopped. The knowledge that the Lord is working today, as He did in times past, to bring persons into His kingdom brings hope and joy to every Christian.

The decline of churches and denominations and the decay of society does not mean the kingdom isn't growing.

Even though some churches and denominations are plateauing and declining, we need to remember that God still is at work in His world and that His kingdom is growing. Jesus Himself gives us this assurance:

" *What is the kingdom of God like, and to what should I compare it? It's like a mustard seed that a man took and sowed in his own garden. It grew and became a tree, and the birds of the sky nested in its branches.' And again He said, 'To what should I compare the kingdom of God? It's like yeast that a woman took and mixed into 50 pounds of flour until it spread through the entire mixture'"* (Luke 13: 18-21).

The failure of people or nations to respond to God does not invalidate for a moment the eternal truths about the growth of God's kingdom.

Jesus inaugurated the growth of God's kingdom on earth.

Jesus spoke the parables of the mustard seed and leaven to a small group of disciples who understood little of who He was, what He taught, and what He did. Christ explained that He inaugurated the kingdom of God among humanity when He began His ministry. God's kingdom was in progress then and has been in progress ever since. Jesus knew the kingdom would grow despite opposition, lack of faith, personal failures, and many other problems.

We discover the secret of kingdom growth and development from God's Word, from history, and from a careful examination of our present circumstances.

THE BEGINNING PLACE FOR GROWTH

We need to begin where God begins. Our Lord set church growth in the arena of the kingdom of God. Within the context of the kingdom, we are able to understand that church growth can and will occur.

Church growth is the result of God's supernatural work through His people to accomplish His kingdom's purposes. Church growth also is the result of God's people obeying His will and His Word in the world.

My prayer is that the kingdom principles of church growth will become your guiding principles and that as you and your church apply them, you will experience church growth as our Lord intended.

I have outlined in a simple, easy-to-remember way the eternal, God-given principles of church growth. These basic principles, mandated by our Lord, have life-changing, church-changing implications and are not difficult to understand.

Church growth results when God's people discover and follow His divinely revealed process of kingdom growth.

1·5·4 PRINCIPLE OF GROWTH

The *1·5·4 Principle* introduced in this book embodies and describes the kingdom process of church growth. If you practice these kingdom principles in your church in the spirit in which our Lord gave them, they offer you and your church the opportunity to experience the power of God working in your church, community, and beyond.

The *1·5·4 Principle* will be repeated often for clarity and to help you understand how each part of the principle fits the whole concept of church growth. The principle involves:

1 driving force for church growth:
   The Great Commission

5 essential church functions for church growth:
   Evangelism
   Discipleship
   Fellowship
   Ministry
   Worship

4 results:
   Numerical Growth
   Spiritual Transformation
   Ministry Expansion
   Kingdom Advance

The *1·5·4 Principle* functions in what our Lord repeatedly calls us to: the kingdom of God.

The opening chapter of this book seeks to place in perspective the essential role of the kingdom of God in church growth.

The next three chapters provide insights into how the Great Commission becomes the *1* driving force of church growth and leads Christians and churches to know and to practice the *5* essential functions and experience the *4* results of church growth. The *1·5·4 Principle* provides an understandable map for churches and church leaders to follow on their journey to the renewed joy of church growth. The last three chapters will show you the practical process for understanding and implementing the *1·5·4 Principle*.

The *1·5·4 Principle* provides you and your church an understandable, easy-to-remember map to the renewed joy of church growth.

THE ESSENTIAL ROLE OF THE KINGDOM OF GOD IN CHURCH GROWTH

T he kingdom of God is the bedrock, the foundation of church growth. It is a dominant theme throughout the New Testament and is the heart of Jesus' preaching. Long before Christ mentioned the church,

"Jesus went to Galilee, preaching the good news of God: 'The time is fulfilled, and the kingdom of God has come near. Repent and believe in the good news!'" (Mark 1:14-15).

Jesus urged His disciples (and us) to pray:

"Our Father in heaven, Your name be honored as holy. Your kingdom come. Your will be done on earth as it is in heaven" (Matt. 6:9-10).

These New Testament Scriptures and more than 70 others speak specifically about the kingdom of God. Numerous other references to "His kingdom," "My kingdom," and "kingdom of heaven" are found throughout the New Testament. Jesus spoke about the kingdom of God on many occasions and taught His disciples its importance. It was the central theme of His preaching. He clearly wants us to understand His kingdom, to pray for its fulfillment, and to be committed participants in its advancement.

Our Lord Invites Believers to Participate in Kingdom Growth

The kingdom of God has many facets. The central idea that permeates the concept is that, in this age, the kingdom is present wherever the will and reign of God is established in people's lives through the presence of Jesus Christ.

God's will for us is to know Him in Christ and to live for Him in such a way that we will realize His purpose for our lives—in this world and for eternity.

THE KINGDOM OF GOD HAS NO LIMITS

The kingdom of God is not geographical, political, or social. It knows no human or earthly limits; neither does it depend on human effort. God has chosen to involve you and me in the advance of His kingdom, but His kingdom rests on His power, not ours. The kingdom of God is, first and foremost, relational. God wants to have a redemptive relationship with us. He wants to reveal Himself to us and to have fellowship with us as He did with Adam and Eve. He establishes and maintains that relationship through the saving grace of Jesus Christ.

NOTHING CAN STOP THE KINGDOM OF GOD

The kingdom is God's. He controls it and moves it according to His plan and will. It grows because He intends for it to grow. Nothing can stop its growth, because nothing can stop God. He builds His church. Nothing can stop Him from building it, because His church is part of His kingdom.

When Peter confessed Jesus as the Messiah of God, Jesus declared:

> *"Blessed are you, Simon son of Jonah, because flesh and blood did not reveal this to you, but My Father in heaven. And I also say to you that you are Peter, and on this rock I will build My church, and the forces of Hades will not overpower it. I will give you the keys of the kingdom of heaven"* *(Matt. 16:17-19).*

God wove His purpose to redeem people from sin into all world history. He intends to call His people out of this world, and nothing can stop Him. The wonderful truth is, He has chosen to use you and me to accomplish His work.

The Lord is at work every day in every place building His kingdom. He is completing that task even though conditions around us might suggest otherwise.

The kingdom of God knows no human or earthly limits.

Nothing can stop the growth of the kingdom and the church, because nothing can stop God.

THE KINGDOM GROWS
REGARDLESS OF THREATS

The kingdom of God has been and is under attack from virtually every direction. Throughout history, God's people have faced challenging obstacles. Experience teaches that churches begin and grow, some decline, and some die. The survival and progress of God's kingdom does not depend on what happens to a church here and there. God always has and always will raise up someone or some agent to carry on His kingdom's work.

Take courage, Christian friends. Your church may be declining, but a vast number are growing. Be faithful; trust God; do your best. Your church's condition may not advance the kingdom in your place, but it does not threaten or destroy the kingdom and its growth. Adverse circumstances in your church may mean that God's kingdom will blossom in other places.

What do you see around your neighborhood and church? Do you see signs of God at work, bringing people to an awareness of Himself and to salvation in Christ? Or do you see declining church attendance, declining baptisms, and fewer church ministries and activities? You may see an increase in crime, violence, divorce, alcoholism, and drug abuse. The moral decay of society may be rising faster than church membership. Your church's financial resources may have dwindled over the years. Your church may be in an urban transitional area or a rural area where population is changing or declining rapidly, greatly reducing your opportunity to grow.

You may be discouraged and wondering how these things relate to Jesus' declaration that the kingdom of God is growing constantly and that the gates of "hell" shall not prevail against it. You and I will be helped as we remember that discouragement and threats are not new. These same kinds of things surrounded Jesus and the disciples of His day. Crime, violence, moral failure, discouragement, spiritual decline, and threats against life never will be removed completely until Jesus returns. These things are evidences of Satan's vicious attacks, but they are not signs that God's kingdom is failing.

What the Lord does is always effective and complete.

> Adverse circumstances in the church and in the world cannot halt the kingdom of God.

13

We cannot measure His work in our world by human standards and our own perceptions.

GOD PRODUCES KINGDOM GROWTH

God is building His kingdom. He is building it on believers who have confessed Jesus Christ as the Son of God, sent to redeem us from our sins (Matt. 16:18-19). He wants to use us to bear His kingdom message—the good news of salvation in Christ—to the world. But never forget, He is the one who produces kingdom growth. Our need is to discover and understand our role in kingdom growth as we join Him in what He is doing in our world.

We need to be aware that the Lord wants us to join Him as He reaches out to redeem persons from sin. No matter how rebellious people are or how sinful they become, God wants to save them from their sin. We are His chosen instruments to accomplish this glorious task.

In good times and in bad times, God constantly is busy at the work of redemption. The Book of Acts is filled with examples of the early church facing oppression, persecution, and death. In spite of this, souls were saved daily and added to the church.

God may be working in the lives of persons around us, even when we cannot seem to reach them. Even when statistics show declines in church attendance, membership, and baptisms, we must not be discouraged. God still is at work. He is more interested in church growth than we are, and He invites us to join Him in the work of redemption.

KINGDOM GROWTH IS LIKE MUSTARD SEED AND LEAVEN

Jesus revealed that the kingdom grows without fanfare or notice. Like a mustard seed in the earth or leaven in bread, the kingdom grows from something barely noticeable to something wonderful and mighty. Regardless of what we think is happening or not happening around us, God is at work growing His kingdom. The heart of that work is bringing men and women to a saving knowledge of Jesus Christ.

> We need to discover and understand our role in what Christ is doing in the kingdom in the world.

> Church growth is rooted in God's purposes to bring His kingdom to fulfillment.

CHURCH GROWTH OCCURS AS THE KINGDOM OF GOD IS FULFILLED

Any understanding of church growth must begin with God's purposes to bring His kingdom to fulfillment. Church growth is not an end in itself. It is part of the larger picture of the advance of the kingdom of God. To focus first and solely on church growth, especially church growth methods, is to lose sight of what God intends for every believer and church.

In our rush to find quick ways to accomplish church growth, we forget that the kingdom of God calls for personal sacrifice, commitment, and giving up our lives for its growth. Many believers seem to have little understanding of the personal sacrifice required by our Lord for kingdom growth, and others are unable or unwilling to pay that price. Jesus reminded His followers:

"If anyone wants to come with Me, he must deny himself, take up his cross daily, and follow Me. For whoever wants to save his life will lose it, but whoever loses his life because of me will save it" (Luke 9:23-24).

Occasionally, a congregation relocates from an older transitional neighborhood to a new area, leaving behind little or no witness to people in the former community. Is it possible that such congregations have an unspoken feeling that God is finished in the old community, that He is no longer at work redeeming persons in that place? Isn't it easier to move than to stay in a transitional neighborhood and sacrifice our lives to win people to the Lord? Whatever feelings we have about such areas, we may be sure that God has not abandoned them; neither should we. God is at work in those places as in other places, building His kingdom; and we ought to stay with Him.

Sometimes churches, in an attempt to breathe new life into their work, spend large amounts of time studying evangelism and ministry. They buy the latest books on the subjects, seek out the latest methods, and wear out cars, buses, and people going to conferences on soul-winning and ministry but never get around to doing the work.

> God never abandons any neighborhood; neither should we.

> Studying evangelism and ministry can never substitute for doing evangelism and ministry.

15

Studying evangelism and ministry is well and good, but study never can substitute for leading unsaved persons to Christ, meeting people's needs, and guiding believers to total commitment to Christ and His kingdom.

WE HAVE NO PROMISE THAT HARDSHIPS WILL CEASE

Jesus spoke frequently of the blessings of the kingdom, but He never suggested that suffering and hardship would cease. On the contrary, He said kingdom growth would require believers to go through trials and struggles. He spoke of opposition, satanic threats, deception, sinful failure, and pressure to quit; but He never promised ease and comfort.

FORTRESS MENTALITY HAS NO PLACE IN THE KINGDOM OF GOD

The kingdom is for everyone. Every believer has a responsibility to reach lost people, wherever they are and in whatever conditions they live.

But before a church can think seriously and correctly about numerical growth, it must understand and address Jesus' teachings on the kingdom of God. Without a commitment to join God in His plan for world redemption, our efforts at church growth are little more than selfish efforts to build fortresses against the attacks of the world and Satan.

The kingdom of God has no place for such a fortress mentality. God did not redeem us to guard His kingdom. Neither does He want us to retreat from threats that surround us. He has given us the ministry and message of reconciliation (2 Cor. 5:18-19) and the power to penetrate our sinful, dark, decadent world with the gospel.

APPLICATION OF KINGDOM PRINCIPLES BRINGS CHURCH GROWTH

Church growth is not a matter of survival; neither is it a way to conserve "our kind" for our churches. Church growth is the application of kingdom principles to local situations, which results in: (1) numerical growth, (2)

Kingdom growth requires struggle and commitment.

God did not redeem us to guard His kingdom or to flee from dangers that surround us.

spiritual transformation, (3) ministry expansion, and (4) kingdom advance. Church growth techniques and methods that fail to include reaching the world from within the membership of a local congregation are destined to be short lived.

Our mission is identical with the early disciples' mission: to preach the kingdom of God. Jesus called His disciples together and gave them power and authority over all devils.

> *"Then He sent them to proclaim the kingdom of God, ...So they went out and traveled from village to village, proclaiming the good news and healing everywhere" (Luke 9:2,6).*

THE CHURCH IS GOD'S AGENT OF REDEMPTION

The church is an important part of the kingdom, but it is not the full kingdom. The church is God's agent of redemption in the world. It is the organism, the instrument God chose to carry His message to the world and to bring people to a saving knowledge of Christ.

The existence of one monolithic, organized institutional church to which everyone belongs is not necessary or even desirable. The Lord has one church, the body of Christ, to which every believer belongs; and that is enough. The variety in kinds of churches and denominations and in church organizational structures within different denominations and churches reflects the freedom and diversity of the body of Christ. In many ways, local church structures are the expression of the members' culture and their understanding from Scripture of what a local congregation should be and do. However, structures that local churches and denominations adopt must be in keeping with God's revealed truth in the Scriptures. No other kind of church can be an effective instrument in His kingdom.

SOUND DOCTRINE IS VITAL TO KINGDOM GROWTH

What Christians and churches believe and teach about the local church and the kingdom of God is vital for a

Our mission is to proclaim the gospel of the kingdom of God to the world.

The variety found in churches and denominations reflects the freedom and diversity of the body of Christ.

KINGDOM PRINCIPLES FOR CHURCH GROWTH

sound application of God's truth to members' lives. To be sure, any doctrine a local church preaches and teaches must conform to God's truth revealed in Scripture.

The essential doctrines that are accepted and believed by most evangelical Christians include the following foundational beliefs:

Jesus Christ is God in the flesh, born of the virgin Mary, come to redeem us from our sin and separation from God.

Jesus assuredly performed the miracles recorded in Scripture.

Jesus died on the cross for our sins and rose from the dead the third day.

Jesus will return bodily to this earth at the end of the age.

The Scriptures are inerrant and completely trustworthy. They were written to lead us to God and salvation through Christ.

CHURCH GROWTH IS THE SUPERNATURAL WORK OF GOD

Christ chose to build His kingdom and church through believers in local congregations doing His will (Matt. 16:18). Church growth occurs as God works through His people to accomplish His purposes and as His people obey His will and His Word.

Church growth is not simply a concept or a method. It is a divinely revealed process built on the will and work of God in the world. The work is God's, but the responsibility to complete it is given to every believer and church.

Our Lord has not left us alone in the world. He is in the world, redeeming the lost, maturing believers, and growing churches. He commissions us to join Him in His kingdom's work and gives us the power to do His will.

> Christ is in the world, redeeming the lost, maturing believers, and growing churches. Let us join Him without delay.

2

ONE GREAT COMMISSION: THE DRIVING FORCE OF CHURCH GROWTH

I n the final days before Jesus ascended to the right hand of the Father, He met His disciples in Galilee and gave them what we know as the Great Commission (Matt. 28:16-20). The Commission is the capstone of the Savior's earthly teaching ministry. It is His ultimate command to evangelize the world, His mandate to His disciples and to every believer.

This powerful message etched itself on the disciples' souls and changed them forever. In the days and years that followed, they preached and taught these life-changing words to early believers. The early churches heard and experienced a power they had never known.

THE CHURCH GREW AS BELIEVERS DID AS THE LORD COMMANDED

The early Christians went from city to city and country to country in the face of intense oppression and difficulty, doing what their Lord had commanded.

Their record of going where no one had gone with the message of redemption has yet to be matched. They saw the lost redeemed. They baptized them, taught them, and shared with them the Lord's incredible promise that He would be with them until the end of the world. Because of these early believers' efforts and God's power, the gospel spread swiftly throughout the known world and has not ceased going to this very day.

The Great Commission has been the driving force of missions and evangelism for believers and churches in every generation since New Testament times. It continues to be the driving force for missions and evangelism and shall ever remain so.

Matthew 28:19-20 is one of the most often quoted passages in the Bible. No two verses of Scripture have been more instrumental in impressing God's call on Christians' hearts to be ministers, missionaries, or committed, witnessing laymen and women. You may have memorized the Great Commission as a child. You may have discovered it right after you were saved or when you were well along in your Christian experience. Usage and familiarity have not reduced the Commission's power to inspire and guide believers in evangelism and world mission.

Jesus Spoke to His Disciples

The church was beginning to grow when Jesus spoke the words recorded in Matthew 28:18-20 to His disciples. The church and kingdom are growing and will continue to grow until He comes. Let us join Him as He reaches out to redeem lost humanity. May we, like the early disciples and believers in every generation since, take to heart Jesus' promise and Commission:

> *Without the driving force of the Great Commission, church growth will be little more than a misguided attempt to gain numbers, discover methods, and do something different.*

"All authority has been given to Me in heaven and on earth. Go, therefore, and make disciples of all nations, baptizing them in the name of the Father and of the Son and of the Holy Spirit, teaching them to observe everything I have commanded you. And remember, I am with you always, to the end of the age" (Matt.28:18-20).

The Great Commission defines God's mission (which is our mission) in the world. The Commission is the Lord's marching orders for every believer and church. Understanding the meaning and full implication of the Commission is crucial if we are to do the work of the church in God's way. The crux of this book is to present the full implication of the Great Commission for church growth in the 21st century.

Without the driving force of the Great Commission, church growth will be little more than a misguided attempt to gain numbers, increase enrollments, discover methods, utilize new marketing techniques, and do something different.

When evangelism, discipleship, and church growth become what we do *for* the Lord rather than what we do *with* the Lord, we quickly lose sight of His mission. God is far more concerned about winning lost people than we are. He has been on mission to redeem lost humanity since the fall of Adam and Eve in the garden of Eden. He is wise in the ways of winning people. If we are wise, we will adopt His way embodied in the Great Commission rather than seeking to devise our own.

We tend to substitute things that are important to us for things that are important to the Lord. Nothing is wrong with techniques, methods, and hard work. Few in the kingdom of God are wearing out from overwork, but many are wearing out from doing things that do not work. We dare not become enamored with the latest techniques and forget the Great Commission. It is the fundamental kingdom principle for church growth. We learn from it what is crucial in church growth, what our Lord expects from us, and what He promises to us. Let us take a fresh look at every aspect of this vital Scripture passage.

> When evangelism, discipleship, and church growth become what we do *for* the Lord rather than what we do *with* the Lord, we quickly lose sight of His mission.

ALL POWER HAS BEEN GIVEN

"All authority has been given to Me in heaven and on earth." — We cannot fulfill the Great Commission in our strength and in our way. The power and authority to do what our Lord has commanded are His, not ours.

Jesus began the church's Commission with a declaration of His power and authority. His power includes all social, spiritual, political, economic, and creative power. Because Jesus is God, He possesses this power and has the right to bestow it on believers and churches.

Christ's power, presence, and authority gives us the courage and the right to go from place to place sharing the good news of salvation. If we did not have His power and His command to share the gospel, our efforts to win persons to Him would be futile. He who rules life, death, the universe, and eternity has instructed us to go into all the world and preach the gospel. Wherever we go, He goes. Wherever He goes, we ought to go.

> The power and authority to do what our Lord commands are His, not ours.

GO

"Go, therefore." — Christ commands us to go into our world with His message of hope and salvation. A church that does not go to lost persons and share the gospel with

them is like a restaurant that has food prepared but refuses to serve the hungry. Believers and churches have no reason to possess Christ's power if they do not share His message with the unsaved.

We do not go to friends, neighbors, and strangers with the gospel primarily because we have a right to go or because we are compelled by our pity for the lost. We go because Christ tells us to go. We are under His orders to go in His power and authority.

Jesus said in the parable of the great supper:

"Go out into the highways and lanes and make them come in, so that my house may be filled" (Luke 14:23).

Following Zacchaeus' conversion, the Savior told him:

"For the Son of Man has come to seek and to save the lost" (Luke 19:10).

We do not need to fear going anywhere to share the gospel. The success we seek is not our own. It is not determined by our worth or abilities. We seek Christ's success, and that success is determined by His will and authority. With that authority, we join Him in His work of redeeming humanity.

The Greek word translated *go* in the Great Commission actually means "as you go" or "since you are going." It focuses on the truth that we always are going somewhere. We are on the move. We do not remain in one place on any given day. We move about, meeting people everywhere who need the Lord.

The second meaning of *go* involves believers going out from their homes and families to other people, nations, and cultures to share the gospel.

From the beginning, the church has been a sending church (Acts 13:1-3). It has sent believers from their cities and countries to take the gospel to people around the world.

We are to go daily and without delay. We are to share Christ with those we see and meet daily. We also are to go to "the ends of the earth" and share the gospel with all

> A church that does not go to lost persons and share the gospel is like a restaurant that has food but refuses to serve the hungry.

people (Acts 1:8). For a Christian, going is not an option; it is the Lord's command.

MAKE DISCIPLES

We need to understand what Jesus meant when He commanded us to teach. The best translation of the Greek word sometimes translated *teach* is "make disciples." To become a disciple, a person has to turn from sin and receive salvation from Christ. The Christian life begins with God's gift of grace and faith to trust in Christ. Salvation is not something a person can do for himself or herself. It comes entirely and only from God.

God Uses Our Witness

When we go into the world and share Christ with others, God uses our witness to save them. Our going and sharing are vitally important but do not save people. God saves them by His grace and gives them the ability to receive Christ by faith (Eph. 2:8-9). When people, aided by the Holy Spirit, repent and turn from their sins to Christ, they become His disciples.

A disciple is a learner, a follower of Christ who has experienced a radical change of life and lifestyle. Disciples give testimony in word and deed that Christ saved them.

Believers and churches are to witness, worship, minister, and work in ways that result in making disciples. This simple concept can be overlooked by those honestly seeking to please the Lord. Whatever my ministry or the ministry of my church, if the fruit of that ministry is not disciples, something is wrong.

Once we understand that only Jesus saves individuals and gives power to change their lives, we are prepared to devote our lives to making disciples. Our Lord brings persons to repentance, faith, and salvation. We are the instruments He uses to accomplish this work.

We Are Partners with God

Our Lord invites us to join Him as His agents in saving the lost from sin. We complement His work by spending time with them: teaching, sharing, and evangelizing them. We are given the wonderful privilege of introduc-

For a Christian, going is not an option; it is the Lord's command.

Our going and sharing are vitally important but do not save people. God saves them by His grace.

23

ing them to Christ. Often these people are not even aware of their need for the Lord. But they can be won because the Lord already is working in their hearts and lives, preparing them to hear the gospel and to be saved.

We are partners with the Lord in redemption. He has chosen us to be His witnesses to tell unsaved persons the good news of salvation. Our task is to give our lives to share the gospel of Christ with every person in the world. We are to pursue every opportunity to share His message. We are to be open to His leadership to go anywhere as His witnesses.

ALL NATIONS

The words *all nations* embodies two important concepts: (1) The kingdom of God is for all people. It is not limited to any racial, national, social, or cultural group. (2) The gospel reveals the Lord's great love for all kinds of persons in all kinds of circumstances in all kinds of places. The tendency of individuals to be nationalistic and prejudiced toward others is a reflection of unregenerate humanity. For the church to narrow the scope of its vision to less than the world is unscriptural.

God created different national and ethnic groups with different languages, customs, and interests. Because He created them, He also wants to redeem them. And that is what He does.

God's heart is not set on saving persons in only one location, region, or nation. He sent Christ to save every person in the world who will believe. Believers' hearts and minds for missions and church growth cannot be less than the Father's. We cannot limit our witness to one location. Believers and churches must have a global vision.

The Unlimited Gospel

The only limits on the gospel, geographic or otherwise, are the ones we put on it in our lives. Many people have little or no understanding of the global dimensions of the gospel. We tend to stay among groups that give us identity and comfort. The Great Commission pushes us to see the world as it really is and to move into that world

For the church to narrow the scope of its vision to less than the world is unscriptural.

Believers' hearts and minds for missions and church growth cannot be less than God's.

with the message of salvation to those in need of redemption.

Unfortunately, some churches limit their methods and strategies to local surroundings. Although no one in those churches would admit to such a limited outlook, the work of the churches reveals it. Their work is limited to their congregations and local areas. Building large congregations without a world view is not scriptural and does not honor Christ who commands us to go to all nations.

From the beginning of the redemptive record, God's message has been a "going" message. When He determined to call out a people for Himself, He first established the nation of Israel. He called Abraham to leave his people and homeland to go to the land of promise to become the ancestor of the Israelites. God said to Abraham:

> *"Get thee out of thy country, and from thy kindred, and from thy father's house, unto a land that I will show thee: And I will make of thee a great nation, and I will bless thee, and make thy name great; and thou shalt be a blessing: and I will bless them that bless thee, and curse him that curseth thee: and in thee shall all families of the earth be blessed"* *(Gen. 12:1-3).*

God also spoke His missionary message through the prophets:

> *"For thou shalt go to all that I shall send thee, and whatsoever I command thee thou shalt speak" (Jer. 1:7).*

Ultimately, God came from heaven to earth in the person of His Son to redeem people from their sin. He commands all His children to go to all people with His message of salvation. With His presence and promise to empower us, God confronts us with His call to reach out to the world with the gospel.

The Great Commission creates a longing in each of us to see every person on earth saved. The passion we have for Christ creates a passion for wanting others to know

> From the beginning of the redemptive record, God's message has been a "going" message.

Him. This can be understood only as the love of Christ controlling our hearts and minds.

God Is at Work Daily Building His Kingdom

God commands us to go into the world and harvest those persons He is calling to Himself. We never have to worry about the availability of lost persons. They are all around us. Neither do we have to wonder if they need the gospel. Jesus said:

"The harvest is abundant, but the workers are few. Therefore, pray to the Lord of the harvest to send out workers into His harvest" (Luke 10:2).

God constantly is preparing persons to receive the message of salvation. They are ripe and ready to be harvested into His kingdom. They may not appear to us to be ready or even willing to hear the gospel. That is not our concern. Our concern is to share the gospel with them and leave the issue of acceptance or rejection with them and the Lord.

People cannot prepare themselves spiritually to receive God's message. Neither are we responsible for making them ready. We are to witness to them, pray for them, love them, and live Christlike lives before them. God alone prepares people's hearts to receive Christ.

FOLLOWING GOD'S EXAMPLE BRINGS CONFIDENCE

Years ago a fresh insight came to me as I read John 5:17. The Jewish religious authorities were criticizing and threatening Jesus for healing on the Sabbath. His answer to those who condemned Him was: "My Father is still working, and I also am working." *The Living Bible* makes the verse's meaning even clearer: "My Father constantly does good, and I'm following his example." A good paraphrase of this statement would be, "My Father is always working, and I join Him."

As these words pierced my heart, a complete freedom and assurance came over me about going to any place to

God commands us to go into the world and harvest those persons He is calling to Himself.

share the gospel. That assurance remains with me until this day. Knowing we are following the Father's example gives us confidence and strength to do His work and will.

Finally, these unsettling, dynamic words, *make disciples of all nations*, mean that we are to go under Christ's command to all nations and make disciples of persons who are not believers. We are to go as far in the world as the Lord leads us. Jesus clearly outlined the church's worldwide mission:

"It is not for you to know times or periods that the Father has set by His own authority. But you will receive power when the Holy Spirit has come upon you, and you will be My witnesses in Jerusalem, in all Judea and Samaria, and to the ends of the earth" (Acts 1:7-8).

What could be clearer and more to the point? Believers have the power of God's Spirit on them to be witnesses for Him in every location in every country around the world.

The words of our Lord ring in our hearts and judge us when we do not obey His command to go to the farthest reaches of the earth.

BAPTIZE
"Baptizing them in the name of the Father and of the Son and of the Holy Spirit."—This statement is a remarkable part of the Great Commission. Who would have thought that baptism would be important enough to be placed in the Great Commission alongside going into all the world to make disciples and teaching them to do what the Lord has commanded? But that is the case. Baptism is an important teaching in the Scriptures and a vital part of the church's effort to make disciples of all nations.

Baptism: An Act of Obedience
We must not lose sight of the meaning and importance of baptism. Jesus commanded it, and His commands are never to be taken lightly. Baptism cannot be set aside for

> Believers have the power of God's Spirit on them to be witnesses for Him in every location in every country around the world.

27

the convenience of those who either do not understand it or cannot be persuaded to be scripturally baptized.

Those who do not want to be baptized may not understand baptism's meaning and importance, or they may not be committed to God and His kingdom. The witnessing believer should spend the time necessary to help such persons understand that his or her salvation experience is to be accompanied by baptism. Believers should wait patiently for these individuals to understand the meaning of baptism and its role in living as disciples. Baptism is an act of obedience and a picture of a person's identification with Christ in His death, burial, and resurrection.

Baptism: Symbol of Redemption

Baptism symbolizes what God has done for us in redemption. When Christ redeems us, we die to sin and rise to new life in Him. Old things, including old desires and lifestyles, pass away and all things become new (2 Cor. 5:17). We are possessed by Christ, who died for us and lives within us. Baptism pictures that spiritual death and resurrection.

Baptism expresses our faith in Christ's literal death, burial, and resurrection and pictures our own coming death, burial, and resurrection. Baptism also pictures our being cleansed from our sins by His blood shed for us on the cross. Finally, baptism is a means by which converts declare publicly their commitment to Christ.

Regardless of people's understanding or misunderstanding of baptism and their feelings about it, the Scriptures direct us to follow Christ in repentance, faith, and believer's baptism. Baptism prepares us for membership in the local church and is an important part of our discipleship when, by God's grace, we have been saved to eternal life.

When we are baptized in the name of the Father, the Son, and the Holy Spirit, we acknowledge that the triune God owns us and that all aspects of our lives are under His control. Baptism is a means of honoring and praising the Lord. Scripturally, our baptism should come at the beginning of our journey with Christ.

> Baptism is an important teaching in the Scriptures and a vital part of the church's effort to make disciples of all nations.

> Baptism is a means by which converts declare publicly their commitment to Christ.

Going to a lost world to make disciples, baptizing them, and teaching them are the heart of the Great Commission. Nothing is unimportant in the Commission. Nothing should be omitted.

TEACHING THEM

"Teaching them to observe everything I have commanded you." — The three commands in the Great Commission — make disciples, baptize them, and teach them — describe our role in fulfilling the Lord's desire to redeem the world.

The commands to make disciples and to teach might appear to be the same, but they are not. *Make disciples* means to make followers of Christ from those who do not know Him. *Teach* means to bring those who are redeemed and baptized into a deeper relationship with Christ and into a better understanding of His will.

Teaching: A Process of Building the Kingdom

Churches are the agents of growth in the kingdom of God. Believers in the churches are the agents of spiritual growth in other believers' lives. Jesus specifically commanded us to teach other believers the things He had commanded us.

Teaching is the process by which the church builds itself up through its members. These members bring life to others by sharing the gospel with them. New believers are baptized in obedience to our Lord's command. Then they are led to spiritual maturity by believers, who help them know and do the things He has commanded.

We cannot take others farther than we have gone with Christ. The Christian life cannot be taught in words alone. We must show others by our actions how the Christian life is lived.

First John 3:18 reminds us:

"Little children, we must not love in word or speech, but in deed and truth."

Nothing is unimportant in the Commission. Nothing should be omitted.

Teach means to bring those who are redeemed and baptized into a deeper relationship with Christ and into a better understanding of His will.

Again, Colossians 3:16-17 declares:

"Let the message about the Messiah dwell richly among you, teaching and admonishing one another in all wisdom, and singing psalms, hymns, and spiritual songs, with gratitude in your hearts to God. And whatever you do, in word or in deed, do everything in the name of the Lord Jesus, giving thanks to God the Father through him."

Teaching Discipleship Takes Time and Patience

Getting people to make a decision for Christ is not easy, but it is easier than discipling them. Discipling others takes time, skill, and patience. It takes commitment to the Lord and to the believers we seek to build up in the faith.

The Christian life cannot be taught in words alone. We must show others how the Christian life is lived by our actions.

Discipling believers is a radical departure from the norm. Giving information is not the only ingredient in teaching people to obey the Lord. We must be willing to go to them where they live and invest the best part of our lives in them. Whatever Christ has done for us in salvation and spiritual growth, we must be willing to share with others who trust Him.

I will have more to say about the process of discipling others later in this book. At this point, I want you to understand that God's plan of redemption includes more than conversion and baptism. God wants believers to be taught how to live, act, and think like Christ. This can only be done on a person-to-person basis. We learn from others how to live as Christians in order to live for Christ ourselves and to teach others how to live for Him. It is God's way and His will for our lives.

Whatever Christ has done for us in salvation and spiritual growth, we must be willing to share with others who trust Him.

I AM WITH YOU

"And remember, I am with you always, to the end of the age." — Can you imagine the disciples reaction when Jesus commissioned them to evangelize the world? He probably saw the looks of amazement and wonder in their faces. Perhaps at that moment Jesus saw the questions in their eyes, wondering whether they actually could do as He commanded.

As a dear friend might do, Jesus looked at them one by one and said, "I am with you always, to the end of the age." They must have taken a deep breath and thought, *He is going to be with us. If He is with us, who can be against us?*

We Are Not Alone

Jesus informed His disciples that His constant presence would be with them to help them fulfill His Commission. He did not give this promise as an afterthought. His promise was intentional and direct. He did not give us marching orders and leave us alone to work things out for ourselves. As we go throughout the world evangelizing, baptizing, and teaching converts, our Lord is beside us, around us, and within us. He alone can redeem persons from sin. We join Him, at His invitation, to live our lives with Him and to give our lives totally and completely to Him.

Time to complete the Great Commission is limited. One day we will have no more time to work at making disciples, baptizing them, and teaching them. The end of the age will come. History will be wrapped up with the coming of Christ from heaven to earth. We will put our tools away and go to stand before our Lord to give an account to Him for our stewardship of the Great Commission.

Empowered to Go to All the World

Christ promises to empower us to go across the world to all persons with the life-changing gospel. Many people will receive our message, because the Lord is at work convicting them and leading them to repentance and faith. We are to lead them into a new life of following Jesus. We also are to baptize them and teach them the things we have learned about Christ.

We cannot succeed in church growth until we understand our role in building the kingdom of God. Church growth occurs when God moves on people's hearts in response to believers carrying out the Great Commission.

Beginning with the things that are outlined clearly in the Great Commission will help churches avoid falling

> Jesus did not give us marching orders and leave us alone to work things out for ourselves.

> Time to complete the Great Commission is limited.

> The Great Commission will help churches avoid falling into the trap of doing *good* things first instead of the *best* things.

into the trap of doing good things first instead of the best things. As important as ministry is, we must direct our energies and attention to the first things our Lord has given us to do. While making disciples, baptizing them, and teaching them usually will go on simultaneously in the church, we must keep our priorities in line with those of the Commission.

FOCUS ON FULFILLING CHRIST'S COMMANDS

We must focus on fulfilling Christ's commands and doing His will reflected in the Great Commission. Otherwise, we will not have the power for church growth that comes through applying the kingdom principles the Lord has given us.

The Great Commission is the *1* in the *1·5·4 Principle* of church growth. Now let us see how *1·5·4* can be implemented in your life and church. The next chapter outlines five things each church must do to grow.

The following chapters will help you understand and apply other kingdom principles of church growth to your life, ministry, and church.

The Great Commission is the *1* in the *1·5·4 Principle* of church growth.

3

FIVE THINGS EACH CHURCH MUST DO TO GROW

Once believers have been part of a growing church, they never are the same. They may not know why their church is growing, but they know they experience excitement and joy in being a part of it. For them, their church is the place to be.

Others experience the opposite. They are members of a church that has plateaued or is declining. They feel the spiritual deadness in their church. They may not even know that their church should or could grow. These church members may have resigned themselves to their situation. They may believe that, for a variety of reasons, such as a changing neighborhood, an aging congregation, or the lack of desire, growth is not possible for their church.

OUR LORD WANTS YOUR CHURCH TO GROW

The contrast between a growing church and one that is not growing is dramatic. The experience of being in a growing church is thrilling; the experience of being in a plateaued or declining church is depressing. Plateaued or declining churches are unnecessarily tragic. Our Lord is eager for every church to grow, and He provides the spiritual power and means to make it happen.

When believers join the Lord in the growth of the kingdom and rely on His power and instructions, their church will begin the invigorating journey of growth.

FIVE FUNCTIONS: THE GATEWAY TO GROWTH

The New Testament outlines five functions every church can and must do in order to fulfill the Great Commission. These five functions may not be new to you; neither will they seem profound. You may have heard these functions so often they have lost their meaning for you. Even so, they produce profound, life-changing effects when they are put into practice. These functions are: *evangelism, discipleship, ministry, fellowship, and worship.*

Simply hearing or reading about these five functions is not enough. They must become active, living principles in our lives before we can experience their God-given power in church growth.

GOD'S WAY OF BUILDING HIS KINGDOM

The Great Commission is God's plan of action for every believer and church. We are to follow Christ's mandate in the Commission until we no longer can work. Its truths will guide our journey in Christ's service until we reach eternity. The Commission's truths may seem rather simple and commonplace. The Lord deliberately made spiritual truths simple to help us know and obey His will (1 Cor. 1:19-21).

Jesus came to earth in response to the Father's will to redeem a people for Himself out of this world. Christ's coming and His death and resurrection are the fulfillment of God's redemptive plan in history. Nothing else can be, needs to be, or will be done to save people from sin.

The Great Commission is God's will expressed to His people in His Word and through His people to the world. God's people are to carry out the Commission as they live and worship Him.

The New Testament contains five functions every church must do corporately to be obedient to the Lord. Each believer must do the same five functions to fulfill his or her calling in the world. As we look at each function, keep in mind that this is God's way of growing churches and building His kingdom in this world.

1. EVANGELISM (ACTS 2:38-41)

No church can grow without evangelism. How can a minister, believer, or church say they believe that salvation can be received only through Jesus Christ in an act of supernatural grace and not share that news with others? To say we believe something as incredible as God's

---

Five essential church functions for church growth are:

Evangelism
Discipleship
Fellowship
Ministry
Worship

The Great Commission is God's will expressed to His people in His Word and through His people to the world.

Acts 2:38-41:

"'Repent,' Peter said to them, 'and be baptized, each of you, in the name of Jesus the Messiah for the forgiveness of your sins, and you will receive the gift of the Holy Spirit. For the promise is for you

(Continued in the next column...)

34

love and then be reluctant to share this good news with others with enthusiasm and joy is beyond belief.

Further, sharing God's good news without the accompanying demands of the gospel is unbelievable. To take the cross of Christ seriously is part and parcel of evangelism. To eliminate the cross is to eliminate the gospel.

EVANGELISM'S CENTER: GOOD NEWS OF THE KINGDOM

The good news of the kingdom of God is the heart of evangelism. Evangelism is what God intended from the beginning (Rev. 13:8). His purpose in the Old Testament was evangelism. He called out Israel, His chosen people, and redeemed them from Egyptian slavery and from Babylonian exile. Certainly, evangelism is God's purpose in the New Testament. That is what He accomplished in Jesus Christ.

Paul reported to the church in Galatia that:

"But when the completion of the time came, God sent His Son, born of a woman, born under the law, to redeem those under the law, so that we might receive adoption as sons" *(Gal. 4:4-5).*

The writer of Hebrews declared:

"Long ago God spoke to the fathers by the prophets at different times and in different ways. In these last days, He has spoken to us by His Son, whom He has appointed heir of all things and through whom He made the universe" *(Heb. 1:1-2).*

NEW TESTAMENT EVANGELISM DEFINED

Christian evangelism is the process of sharing the gospel with lost persons and winning people to Christ enabling them to enter the kingdom of God. It is asking them to repent of their sins, to put their faith in Christ for the forgiveness of sins and the free gift of eternal life, and to follow Him forever as Lord. Evangelism is the good news spoken by believers and lived out in their lives.

The leaders and members of the early Jerusalem church rejoiced that:

and for your children, and for all who are far off, as many as the Lord our God will call.' And with many other words he testified and strongly urged them, saying, 'Be saved from this corrupt generation!' So those who accepted his message were baptized, and that day about three thousand people were added to them" (Acts 2:38-41).

To take the cross of Christ seriously is part and parcel of evangelism. To eliminate the cross is to eliminate the gospel.

Evangelism is the good news spoken by believers and lived out in their lives.

"They were counted worthy to be dishonored on behalf of the name. Every day in the temple complex, and in various homes, they continued teaching and proclaiming the good news that the Messiah is Jesus" (Acts 5:41-42).

These early believers considered it their responsibility and privilege to share the message of salvation. Persecution and fear did not silence them. Neither was God's power lessened. These devoted followers of Christ became models for modern-day evangelism.

During this period, our Lord confronted Saul of Tarsus with his sins. Ananias, an early believer, witnessed to Saul. Saul, who persecuted Christians, became Paul the missionary evangelist, who so effectively preached the saving grace and power of Jesus Christ.

The evangelistic efforts of early Christians spread the gospel throughout the regions of Judea and Samaria, to the surrounding territories, and eventually to the known world. To this very hour, evangelism is a God-given function for church and kingdom growth.

> Evangelism is a God-given function of the church for church and kingdom growth.

MESSAGE MORE IMPORTANT THAN METHODS

Evangelistic methods are important, but not as important as the gospel. How we present the gospel is important, but not as important as the need to share the gospel with others. We may prefer to build a relationship with persons to whom we want to witness, or we may be comfortable sharing our witness with total strangers. In any case, the gospel must be shared with every person possible as soon as possible. In fact, our comfort zone is of little consequence compared to the need to share the gospel with lost persons.

> The gospel must be shared with every person possible as soon as possible.

Unfortunately, we discuss and argue over methods while persons around us perish. The *how* never can take the place of the *why* in witnessing.

SAVED TO EVANGELIZE OTHERS

We are saved to evangelize the lost. Evangelism is not just a belief; it is spiritual interaction between saved persons and lost persons. We are not evangelistic simply because we believe the gospel or have a burden for those who are lost in sin. We are not evangelistic even when we study the gospel or receive training in sharing our testimonies and in making a gospel presentation. We are evangelistic only when we share the gospel and our faith in Jesus Christ with others who do not know Him as Lord and Savior.

Paul reminds us that God has saved us and given us the ministry of reconciliation:

"Now everything is from God, who reconciled us to Himself through Christ and gave us the ministry of reconciliation: that is, in Christ, God was reconciling the world to Himself, not counting their trespasses against them, and He has committed the message of reconciliation to us" (2 Cor. 5:18-19).

WE MUST JOIN OUR LORD IN EVANGELIZING EVERY PERSON

We are saved from our sin and separation from God, in part at least, to become involved in His work of reconciling lost persons to Himself. God's mission is to redeem people from sin. His method is for believers to share the redemptive Word and to do the ministry of redemption in this world.

Because God has chosen to redeem people from sin, we must join Him by seeking to evangelize every person in the world. If we fail to evangelize persons separated from God, we fail to obey Him, and we fail to join Him in what He wants believers and churches to do.

RECORDS REVEAL FAILURE TO EVANGELIZE

Statistics in denominational handbooks, state convention and associational reports, and church records sadden caring persons when they see the low number of baptisms recorded by many churches.

As the world's population grows and the Lord works to redeem lost persons, more Christians and more churches seem to do less evangelism. Baptisms are certainly not the only measure of church growth, but sadly, recorded conversions are not keeping pace with population growth.

> We are evangelistic only when we share our faith in Jesus Christ with others who do not know Him as Lord and Savior.

> Because God has chosen to redeem people from sin, we must join Him by seeking to evangelize every person in the world.

Evangelism: Essential Function for Church Growth

We must never replace evangelism with anything else. Everything we do individually and corporately in the church ultimately should be a witness to lost people and work toward making them disciples. When this is not the case, no legitimate church growth can occur, no matter how busy we are and how much we seem to accomplish. Paul reminded us of the importance of evangelism when he declared:

"For if I preach the gospel, I have no reason to boast, because an obligation is placed on me. And woe to me if I do not preach the gospel!" (1 Cor. 9:16).

Every Christian is responsible for declaring the good news of Christ's coming and His death, burial, resurrection, and return. If we do not, we will give an account to the Father. The manner of delivering the message is not the crucial point. The responsibility for delivering the message is the decisive issue.

Evangelism under the lordship of Christ is the only way to make disciples. Whatever else churches do, they must make disciples. Evangelism is unique in that the need for the gospel is universal and the message is universal and effective in all cultures. Evangelism is a believer sharing the gospel with a lost person in ways both understand.

Believers Are Responsible for Sharing Salvation's Message

"So faith comes from what is heard, and what is heard comes through the message about Christ" (Rom. 10:17).

Our responsibility is to share the Word with those who have not heard it or who have not responded to it. The Word has inherent power to bring people to Christ for salvation (Isa. 55:11).

How fitting that God should choose saved sinners to share the gospel! Only the redeemed understand separation and salvation. We know what it is like to be lost and

> Everything we do individually and corporately in the church ultimately should be a witness to lost people and work toward making them disciples.

> The Word has inherent power to bring people to Christ for salvation.

to be saved. We know what it is like to be softened through the convicting power of the Holy Spirit to receive the gospel. We know what it is like to hear the gospel from another person, and we know what it is like to respond to the gospel. We know what it is like to repent of sins and to trust Christ. We know what it means to become a disciple and to be baptized into a local church. Even angels have not had those experiences and are not equipped to witness to lost persons.

EVANGELISM: A KINGDOM PRINCIPLE FOR GROWTH

We are God's method for evangelizing the world. He has no other. We are His plan, and our obedience means growth in the kingdom and in the churches where we worship and serve. God saves us to send us into the world to speak, live, and show His good news of salvation to persons separated from Him. That is evangelism: the first kingdom principle of church growth.

2. DISCIPLESHIP (ACTS 2:42-43)

The second church function for growth is as familiar and important as the first. This second kingdom principle — discipleship — is much talked about but probably is practiced the least of all church functions.

Discipleship is a lifelong journey of obedience to Christ that transforms a person's values and behavior and results in ministry in one's home, church, and the world. Discipling is the process of teaching the new citizen in the kingdom of God to love, trust, and obey God the King and how to win and train others to do the same.

Churches and individual believers seem to show great interest in discipleship. That interest is evidenced by the increasing number of books, articles, and conferences that promote and teach discipleship. Many people are genuinely concerned about its importance in churches today.

Unfortunately, we have more talk than action about discipleship. The reason may be that to practice discipleship calls for our undivided attention and total commitment to follow the commands of our Lord.

Discipleship is a process that begins after conversion and continues throughout a believer's life.

Discipleship calls for our undivided attention and commitment to follow the commands of our Lord.

Acts 2:42-43:

"And they devoted themselves to the apostles' teaching, to fellowship, to the breaking of bread, and to prayers. Then fear came over everyone, and many wonders and signs were being performed through the apostles" (Acts 2:42-43).

DISCIPLESHIP IS NOT AN OPTION

Discipleship is not an option for any church or believer. Christ mandated it in the Great Commission. The Father's will and a requirement for growing the kingdom is for believers to disciple one another. To disciple others is to obey our Lord's command; to do otherwise is to disobey Him.

Jesus did everything possible to teach and to show us in word and in deed how costly the kingdom would be for us:

> *"If anyone wants to come with Me, he must deny himself, take up his cross daily, and follow Me. For whoever wants to save his life will lose it, but whoever loses his life because of Me will save it" (Luke 9:23-24).*

DISCIPLESHIP IS A KINGDOM PRINCIPLE

Discipleship is to be undertaken with a seriousness and an intensity rarely understood and practiced in the modern church or in the lives of believers. To practice discipleship is to discover a kingdom principle of church growth as well as personal giftedness and spiritual growth.

To understand that discipleship is not an option for believers and that it involves taking up one's cross daily to follow Christ is to begin to understand the work of each believer and church.

DISCIPLESHIP'S FAMOUS PASSAGE

Paul, in the most famous passage on discipleship ever written, stated:

> *"And He personally gave some to be apostles, some prophets, some evangelists, some pastors and teachers, for the training of the saints in the work of ministry, to build up the body of Christ, until we all reach unity in the faith and in the knowledge of God's Son, growing into a mature man with a stature measured by Christ's fullness. Then we will no longer be little children, tossed by the waves and blown around by every wind of teaching, by human cunning with cleverness in the techniques of deceit. But speaking the truth*

The Father's will is for believers to disciple one another.

Discipleship involves taking up one's cross daily to follow Christ.

in love, let us grow in every way into Him who is the Head — Christ" (Eph. 4:11-15).

This passage perfectly expresses God's will for every believer as He builds His kingdom. He calls and appoints persons with special gifts to equip the saints for their work in building up the body of Christ. Sadly, many churches do little to disciple believers when our Lord is ready and willing to guide and empower us to accomplish the task.

Mature discipleship means that believers are living for the Lord in all areas of life. They take the Bible seriously and without question or compromise. The life of Christ is the center and focus of their lives.

HOLINESS IS A REALITY FOR BELIEVERS

Holiness is not just a topic for debate or discussion. It is the center of Christlikeness. It is a reality in believers' lives. They have been set apart by God for kingdom service and are to live separated lives as Christ's disciples. Such discipleship often is neglected in churches because of Christ's high demands and the difficulty of the discipling process.

Discipleship produces something in believers' lives that causes them to think and behave like Christ. Can you imagine Christ living a compromised life? Can you imagine Him doubting the truth of the Father's commands or failing to count the cost of being in the kingdom of God? As believers become more like Christ, the uncompromised life becomes a way of life. Paul reminded us of such a life:

"More than that, I also consider everything to be a loss in view of the surpassing value of knowing Christ Jesus my Lord. Because of Him I have suffered the loss of all things and consider them filth, so that I may gain Christ" (Phil. 3:8).

Peter provides us more insight into such a life and its effect on our daily living:

"Therefore, since Christ suffered in the flesh, arm your-

> Mature discipleship means that believers are living for the Lord in all areas of life.

> As believers become more like Christ, the uncompromised life becomes a way of life.

selves also with the same resolve — because the One who suffered in the flesh has finished with sin — in order to live the remaining time in the flesh, no longer for human desires, but for God's will" (1 Pet. 4:1-2).

Salvation leads to a life of discipleship filled with struggles, dangers, inconvenience, and suffering; but it is accompanied by God's presence and brings us everlasting joy and fulfillment.

THE DIFFERENT KINGDOM PRINCIPLE

The kingdom principle of discipleship is very different from the message we often hear today: a message that extols the benefits of selfish pursuits in life, regardless of what the Scriptures say or mean. Jesus does not call us to a life of ease and comfort. He calls us to seek the kingdom of God first, with the understanding that the Father will provide whatever we need.

Nothing about the Christian life is natural or easy. We must be taught to understand and practice the ways of Christ. We must see kingdom living displayed in believers who are more spiritually mature than we. Then we must model kingdom living for those who are younger in their faith in Christ than we. The influence of more mature believers on younger Christians in the discipling process is immeasurably important.

GOD'S PLAN FOR MATURITY

Discipleship is God's plan for maturing His children. We are saved by God through His grace and given to the church for care and nurture. Discipling believers requires commitment, patience, and obedience, because growing and maturing believers requires time. It is the hardest task the church accomplishes.

PERSONAL RESPONSIBILITY FOR DISCIPLING OUR FAMILIES

Discipleship has a personal dimension that often is neglected. Believers have a responsibility for discipling others in their church. Believers have an additional personal responsibility for discipling those to whom they are

Jesus calls us to seek God's kingdom first.

Discipling believers requires commitment, patience, and obedience.

closely related. From the days of Israel's exodus from Egypt to the present, God's people have had a personal responsibility to disciple their family members. Moses said to the fathers in Israel:

"Hear, O Israel: The Lord our God is one Lord: And thou shalt love the Lord thy God with all thine heart, and with all thy soul, and with all thy might. And these words, which I command thee this day, shall be in thine heart: And thou shalt teach them diligently unto thy children, and shalt talk of them when thou sittest in thine house, and when thou walkest by the way, and when thou liest down, and when thou risest up" (Deut. 6:4-7).

For me, discipleship begins with myself. Then it moves to my family and on to my extended sphere of Christian influence. As I support discipleship in my church, I cannot neglect it in my own life, my family, and with other believers with whom I have influence.

> As I support discipleship in my church, I cannot neglect it in my own life and in my family.

I must obey Christ and learn of Him in my life. If I omit discipleship from my life, my needs for spiritual growth and maturity are not met and I forfeit my right to disciple others. I cannot mature as a Christian by myself. I need the sure instruction of God's Word taught by patient, gifted teachers in the church. I also need the nurture of the church's fellowship and ministry.

> If I omit discipleship from my life, my needs for spiritual growth and maturity are not met and I forfeit my right to disciple others.

I cannot turn over the discipling of my family to someone else. If my church does or does not disciple my family, I have a responsibility to model Christian living before my children and other family members. I have a duty to teach them the things of Christ.

Parents are to bring up their children in the nurture and admonition of the Lord so that they may receive Christ and grow in faith and in obedience to Him. Parents need the help, support, and resources of their local church, but churches cannot relieve parents of their responsibility for discipling their children.

> Churches cannot relieve parents of their responsibility for discipling their children.

KINGDOM PRINCIPLE WITH THE STRONGEST DEMANDS

Discipleship is the kingdom principle of church growth

KINGDOM PRINCIPLES FOR CHURCH GROWTH

that makes the strongest demands on believers and churches. Jesus commanded us in the Great Commission to make disciples of unbelievers throughout the world, to baptize the new converts, and to disciple them in the Christian faith. We are to give our lives to world evangelism and to discipling believers. We have no greater commitment to God than to be willing to go anywhere to fulfill His mission of world redemption through evangelism and discipleship.

3. FELLOWSHIP (ACTS 2:42, 46-47)

The kingdom principle of fellowship is a companion to evangelism, discipleship, and ministry. Fellowship does not happen by accident. It does not happen without the power of God working in individual believers and in the church body. As believers share with others their salvation experiences, practice living Christlike lives, and demonstrate their faith by serving others, fellowship flourishes as surely as summer follows spring.

Fellowship is more than just a feeling of goodwill in a congregation. Fellowship is the intimate spiritual relationship that Christians share with God and other believers through their relationship with Jesus Christ.

GOD'S COVENANT WITH HIS PEOPLE

In the Old Testament, the essential religious unit was the spiritual community of Israel, the people of God. Moses announced at Mount Sinai: "The Lord our God made a covenant with us" (Deut. 5:2) as he presented the Ten Commandments to Israel. As a group and as individuals, God's people shared this covenant because they were the redeemed community.

Jeremiah spoke of God's covenant with the house of Israel. Ezekiel identified Israel as a new community of the Spirit. Daniel wrote about the saints of the Most High. God was present in the lives of these people, and they were keenly aware of it.

The ark of the covenant and the temple were symbols of God's presence with Israel and were reminders of His covenant with them.

Acts 2:42, 46-47:

"And they devoted themselves to the apostles' teaching, to fellowship, to the breaking of bread, and to prayers. And every day they devoted themselves to meeting together in the temple complex, and broke bread from house to house. They ate their food with gladness and simplicity of heart, praising God and having favor with all the people. And every day the Lord added those being saved to them" (Acts 2:42, 46-47).

GOD'S NEW COVENANT IN JESUS

Jesus came announcing the New Covenant. Those who received Him were "in Christ." After the coming of the Holy Spirit at Pentecost, a unique fellowship came together and the followers of our Lord "devoted themselves to the apostles' teaching, to fellowship, to the breaking of bread, and to prayers" (Acts 2:42).

That wonderful New Testament term for fellowship (*koinonia*) appears in this passage. The Greek word *koinonia* is one of the familiar concepts in the New Testament. The word means "to share in," "to come into communion," "to come into fellowship." It appears in our words *communion* and *community*.

FELLOWSHIP AND THE LORD'S SUPPER

Jesus gave the Lord's Supper to the church as a family fellowship event to be observed in remembrance of Him (Luke 22:19). This Memorial Supper symbolizes the sacrifice Christ made for us on the cross (1 Cor. 11:26) and serves as a striking reminder of His eternal presence with the fellowship of believers until He returns.

Paul warned the church at Corinth, whose fellowship was broken through divisions, disputes, and selfishness, that they were endangering the welfare of the church by their abuses of the Lord's Supper. Paul declared that a church in that condition could not partake properly of the Lord's Supper (1 Cor. 11:17-20). He urged those early believers to take the observance of the Lord's Supper seriously and warned them that such crude fellowship violations at the Lord's Supper could result in disaster for the church (1 Cor. 11:27-30). He instructed them that if they ate and drank of the Supper in such an unworthy manner, they were guilty of sinning against the body and blood of the Lord. The apostle urged:

"So a man should examine himself; in this way he should eat of the bread and drink of the cup. For whoever eats and drinks without recognizing the body, eats and drinks judgment on himself. This is why many are sick and ill among you, and many have fallen asleep." (1 Cor. 11:28-30).

> After the coming of the Holy Spirit at Pentecost, a unique fellowship came together.

> The Greek word *koinonia*, translated "fellowship," means "to share in," "to come into communion," "to come into fellowship."

FELLOWSHIP: A KEY TO CHURCH GROWTH

The kingdom principle of fellowship is vital to church growth. Without warm, loving fellowship churches will not grow. People will not come where bickering, selfishness, coldness, and tensions prevail. Who can blame them? People want to be where peace, joy, love, and family relationships prevail.

The fellowship principle goes hand in hand with the other 1·5·4 principles. First comes evangelism; then comes discipleship and ministry. Emerging out of these essential functions comes fellowship, which is a vital part of worship.

The reason for broken church fellowship usually is not hard to find. A church whose fellowship is broken usually is a church that has lost sight of its other main functions — evangelism, discipleship, ministry, and worship — and is out of fellowship with the Lord. Churches cannot have the kind of fellowship we want and our Lord expects unless they focus on evangelism, discipleship, ministry, and worship. A church whose fellowship is broken needs only to return to these functions to restore fellowship among its members.

First John 1:6-7 points out that:

"If we say, 'We have fellowship with Him,' and walk in darkness, we are lying and are not practicing the truth. But if we walk in the light as He Himself is in the light, we have fellowship with one another, and the blood of Jesus His Son cleanses us from all sin."

Is it any wonder that, for many churches, growth is more a dream than a reality? What church leader could not testify to what happens when the church's fellowship is broken? When the church's fellowship is in tatters, you can be sure the other kingdom principles are being neglected.

Just as evangelism is a prerequisite to discipleship and ministry, fellowship follows naturally when a church heeds God's call to practice the other four kingdom principles.

The fellowship principle goes hand in hand with the other 1·5·4 principles.

A church whose fellowship is broken usually is a church that has lost sight of its other main functions — evangelism, discipleship, ministry, and worship.

Fellowship follows naturally when a church heeds God's call to practice the other four kingdom principles.

FELLOWSHIP BEGINS WITH SALVATION

We are to set our sights on the Lord. We are to remember that God has called us out of our sin and our separation from Him to become His children. We have received grace and mercy from a holy, loving Father, who placed the pain and punishment of our sins on Jesus Christ, His Son.

MEMBERS OF GOD'S FAMILY

When we receive Christ we become part of a living fellowship of others who, like us, have been called out. The Father places us in His family and gives us new brothers and sisters in Christ for eternity.

When we receive Christ, we become members of one another and part of a great family of believers across the world, across time, and for eternity. The church is a body of believers saved by grace through faith in Christ Jesus. Believers share a bond in Christ that is unique and distinguishes our relationships from any other group in the world.

The early church experienced fellowship and witnessed what could happen when this kingdom principle is practiced. The Scripture reports:

"So those who accepted his message were baptized, and that day about three thousand people were added to them. And they devoted themselves to the apostles' teaching, to fellowship, to the breaking of bread, and to prayers" (Acts 2:41-42).

> Believers share a bond in Christ that is unique and distinguishes our relationships from any other group in the world.

BECOME ONE WITH CHRIST

Jesus described His relationship with the Father in terms of oneness (John 10:30) and offered us that same kind of relationship with Him and with one another. He prayed just before His crucifixion:

"May they all be one, just as You, Father, are in Me and I am in You. May they also be one in Us, so that the world may believe You sent Me" (John 17:21).

Christ's unity with the Father is a pattern for us to display and enjoy in the church. Without Christian unity, the world will have little respect for our witness. Jesus said:

> Christ's unity with the Father is a pattern for us to display and enjoy in the church.

"By this all people will know that you are My disciples, if you have love for one another" (John 13:35).

UNITY OF FELLOWSHIP IS PRODUCED BY GOD'S LOVE

The church is bound together not with creeds or confessions, not with programs and ministries, but with a unity produced by the Holy Spirit and driven by God's love for us and our love for Him and one another. Jesus declared:

"I give you a new commandment: that you love one another. Just as I have loved you, you should also love one another" (John 13:34).

The fulfillment of the Great Commission hinges on our fellowship as well as on our evangelistic efforts, our discipleship commitments, and our ministries. Paul urged his Ephesian readers:

"With all humility and gentleness, with patience, accepting one another in love, diligently keeping the unity of the Spirit with the peace that binds us" (Eph. 4:2-3).

WHEN UNITY IS ABSENT, GOD IS NOT IN CHARGE

The church is blessed with the ministry of the Holy Spirit. The Spirit convicts us of sins and makes us alive forever in Jesus. He gifts us to do ministry. He produces spiritual fruit to build our lives together. He thus creates a church that is supernatural. If unity is absent from a local church, the Holy Spirit is not in charge.

FELLOWSHIP AS "FAMILYSHIP"

The work of Christ and the Spirit in our lives gives us love for one another and a unity of purpose and vision. This results in fellowship. Fellowship in the Spirit allows us to be part of God's family. In fact, fellowship might be called "familyship." The church is a family of believers. We belong to one another and to the Father. We are part of a larger family that stretches across time into eternity.

The fulfillment of the Great Commission hinges on our fellowship as well as on our evangelistic efforts, our discipleship commitments, and our ministries.

If unity is absent from a local church, the Holy Spirit is not in charge.

The church is a family of believers. Fellowship might be called "familyship."

We are linked to saints of the Old and New Testaments and to people not yet born whom Christ will redeem in days to come.

WHY IS FELLOWSHIP FORGOTTEN?

With all the concern shown to churches, believers, and their ministries today, why do we have such an absence of concern for fellowship? How many believers truly understand the nature of the church as a fellowship or a "familyship"? Somehow we are more aware of fellowship when it does not exist than when it does. Do we assume fellowship occurs automatically without our working at building it? Have we gotten in such a headlong rush trying to do church and to fulfill our own agendas that we have lost our vision of the need to build a strong fellowship?

FELLOWSHIP BONDS BELIEVERS IN LOVE AND UNITY

We spend far too little time building fellowship compared to doing the other functions of the church. Some even suggest fellowship is a by-product of the other functions. While evangelism, discipleship, ministry, and worship are extremely important, they cannot be done effectively without a strong, loving Christian fellowship. The time Jesus spent modeling love, unity, and sharing with His disciples underscores the importance of fellowship.

If anyone chooses to believe evangelism, discipleship, ministry, and worship are the essential functions of the church, that person must believe that fellowship is the incubator for their success. Think of the times Jesus and His disciples and Paul and the early churches met to share meals, to spend time together, and to display their love and commitment to one another.

Fellowship is far more than eating a meal together or going on a trip with other believers. It is more than having a party at the church or someone's house. Fellowship may occur at these events, but fellowship is an essential function of the church. Fellowship is the way members of a church express the "oneness" they share in Christ. It is generated by the Holy Spirit, by God's love for us, and

Have we gotten in such a headlong rush trying to do church and to fulfill our own agendas that we have lost our vision of the need to build a strong fellowship?

Evangelism, discipleship, ministry, and worship cannot be done effectively without a strong, loving fellowship.

by our love for Him and one another. Fellowship bonds the family of God together in love and unity.

CHRISTIAN FELLOWSHIP IS UNIQUE IN THE WORLD

Much is lost when fellowship is not built, and much more is gained than can be imagined when it is built. The bond of Christ in God's family is there to enrich, strengthen, heal, uplift, and to give us a vision of what the Christian family can be at its best.

When one Christian meets another anywhere in the world, regardless of language, color, or culture, they have an immediate bond with each other because they share the same saving grace of Jesus Christ and their faith in the Lord. Believers share such common experiences with one another as conviction, salvation, God's leadership, receiving gifts for ministry, the presence of the Spirit, and bearing spiritual fruit.

For all these reasons and more, the bond of Christian fellowship must be developed to its highest potential in our lives and churches.

CHRISTIAN FELLOWSHIP: A DIVINE GIFT TO CHURCHES

Fellowship needs to be appreciated for its incredible value and needs to be developed to make churches we serve better and more effective. God's kingdom is built as much on scriptural fellowship as anything else.

Jesus Christ prayed for our unity in John 17. John declared that his purpose for writing his First Epistle was to bring people into fellowship with the Father and Son and with believers in the church.

"What we have seen and heard we also declare to you, so that you may have fellowship with us; and indeed our fellowship is with the Father and with his Son Jesus Christ" (1 John 1:3).

GROWTH FLOURISHES AS FELLOWSHIP INCREASES

How much more evangelism would we do if we longed to have fellowship with lost humanity? When we experi-

---

Fellowship bonds the family of God together in love and unity.

Fellowship gives us a taste of what the family of God is like now and will be like in heaven.

ence the kind of fellowship our Lord intended, our view of people now living in sin and under the power of Satan changes dramatically. Our motivation to reach them with the gospel is stimulated and heightened.

Fellowship allows believers to experience the richness of human and divine relationships in time and points them to eternity when we will live together with Jesus forever. Fellowship enables us to experience God's family now and gives us a taste of what the family will be like in heaven. The desire for fellowship is the mark of a mature believer and a mature congregation.

FELLOWSHIP: A KINGDOM PRINCIPLE OF CHURCH GROWTH

Fellowship is an essential function of the church and a key to the church aggressively fulfilling the Great Commission. Our fellowship with the Lord, our life in the Spirit, and our relationships with one another motivate us to reach, teach, and win others to Christ.

The fellowship of the church provides an atmosphere in which believers can mature and be nourished. Without this fellowship and our accountability to the Lord and other believers, we might be tempted to live our lives away from Him and apart from other believers.

A church which practices New Testament fellowship cares for its members and watches to see if they are drifting away from their commitments to Christ. The love of Christ moves us to those in our number who struggle and have needs. A good church fellowship watches over its members and ministers to them when needs arise.

Building relationships of interdependence, evangelizing the lost, and caring for one another are the hallmarks of the kingdom principle of fellowship.

"When James, Cephas, and John, recognized as pillars, acknowledged the grace that had been given to me, they gave the right hand of fellowship to me and Barnabas, agreeing that we should go to the Gentiles" (Gal. 2:9).

In Paul's first and second letter to the church at Corinth, he wrote:

Fellowship is an essential function of the church and a key to the church aggressively fulfilling the Great Commission.

Building relationships of interdependence, evangelizing the lost, and caring for one another are the hallmarks of the kingdom principle of fellowship.

"God is faithful; by Him you were called into fellowship with His Son, Jesus Christ our Lord" (1 Cor. 1:9).

"They begged us insistently for the privilege of sharing in the ministry to the saints, and not just as we had hoped. Instead, they gave themselves especially to the Lord, then to us by God's will" (2 Cor. 8:4-5).

Without the principle of fellowship in operation, churches find it difficult if not impossible to practice the fifth essential function of the church: worship. Churches where the fellowship is fractured and tensions run high or spiritual depression has set in will do little in evangelism, discipleship, ministry, or worship.

4. MINISTRY (ACTS 2:44-45)

This kingdom principle of church growth is rooted in the compassion and concern the Lord builds into our hearts when we enter His kingdom.

Ministry is a kingdom principle and a God-given function of the church. Ministry naturally follows evangelism and discipleship in the Christian developmental process. Of course, evangelism, discipleship, and ministry probably will be occurring simultaneously in the church. Churches usually do not do evangelism, then discipleship, and then ministry. But ministry grows out of a transformed and serving life. Ministry is meeting another person's need in the name of Jesus, expressed as service to persons inside the church family and expressed as missions to persons outside the church. Jesus reminded us:

"Whoever wants to become great among you must be your servant, and whoever wants to be first among you must be your slave; just as the Son of Man did not come to be served, but to serve, and to give His life — a ransom for many" (Matt. 20:26-28).

Paul explained to the church at Ephesus that they were to equip or disciple the saints to do the work of ministry. Ministry or service cannot be separated from evangelism and discipleship. All ministry that is Christian ultimately is evangelistic, and ministering aids in maturing believers. Jesus did not separate doing good and doing God's will.

Early believers got involved in helping ministries because Jesus had changed their lives. Whatever good the early church did was done in the name of Jesus and for God's glory. Persons who do good things without relating them to Jesus Christ are not doing Christian ministry.

Prerequisites to Ministry

Evangelism and discipleship are prerequisites to ministry in the sequence God uses to build His kingdom. Believers and churches often have tried to achieve balance between evangelism and ministry. That is not a problem. Only when we do not recognize the logical progression of these functions in the Great Commission do we put them in opposition to one another or invert their biblical order. Ministry and evangelism are linked to one another as firmly as discipleship and evangelism.

This logical priority leads us to conclude that a person's spiritual needs are more important than his or her physical needs. Persons' physical needs are vitally important, but their relationship with the Lord is paramount. Moses declared:

"Man doth not live by bread only, but by every word that proceedeth out of the mouth of the Lord doth man live" (Deut. 8:3).

At times, God allowed the Israelites to go without food and water on their journey from Egypt to the promised land. This tested their loyalty to Him and taught the valuable lesson that people's relationship with the Lord takes precedence over even food and water.

When Jesus, in spite of His hunger, refused food during the temptations in the wilderness, He quoted Deuteronomy 8:3 (see Luke 4:4).

Persons are separated from God until they are redeemed by His grace in Christ. Ministry to these individuals needs to be accompanied by a Christian witness and needs to focus on their salvation as the ultimate goal of Christian ministry.

> All ministry that is Christian ultimately is evangelistic.

> Evangelism and discipleship are prerequisites to ministry.

> Ministry and evangelism are linked to one another as firmly as discipleship and evangelism.

CALLED TO MINISTRY

Believers are not excused from ministry because evangelism is primary in the Great Commission. Ministry cannot replace evangelism in importance, but ministry is an essential function of a growing church. In fact, we are called to ministry by Christ, the ultimate Minister.

What is the proper place of ministry in the church and in the Christian life? If we keep in mind that the Father is redeeming persons of His choosing out of the world and building His kingdom, ministry's role in kingdom and church growth becomes evident.

Christian compassion and the principles of God's kingdom demand that we minister to all persons without regard to their race, religious affiliation, abilities, or circumstances. We meet the needs of others in response to the command of Christ. If we fail to minister, we fail to obey the Lord's command. In eternity, we will find we have ministered to Jesus as we have ministered to needy, hurting persons. He said:

"I assure you: Whatever you did for one of the least of these brothers of Mine, you did for Me" (Matt. 25:40).

Ministry is an important function of the church. It probably is the best understood and most practiced of the five functions considered in this book. Ministry, however, runs much deeper than we might first realize. God, who is sovereign and controls all things in His creation, has not chosen to remove poverty, disease, war, and other sin-produced scourges from this earth until world redemption is complete (Rom. 8:18-23).

Jesus reminded His disciples:

"You always have the poor with you, and you can do good for them whenever you want, but you do not always have Me" (Mark 14:7).

The Savior was not giving us an excuse for failing to minister to poor, needy, hurting people. On the contrary, He was pointing out the constant need to minister to them with the resources God provides.

> Ministry is an essential function of a growing church.

> Ministry probably is the best understood and most practiced of the five functions considered in this book.

GOD PROVIDES MEANS AND POWER TO MINISTER

Christians may view ministry as something they can do in their own power and with their own resources. We cannot save persons in our own power. Neither can we adequately meet their needs. Only God can provide the means to minister to the overwhelming needs of persons worldwide. Human need is so staggering in our world today that all available human resources are not enough to meet them. We desperately need God's help and blessing in this huge task. Christian ministry needs God's blessings so that our efforts will result in meeting persons' needs and in winning the unsaved to Christ.

Christian ministry is a part of our stewardship as we live for the Lord and serve Him. We do not own anything. We are stewards of what God gives us. Helpless, hurting persons are our responsibility. We are to help and love them in the name of Christ with the resources He provides. Persons' physical and spiritual needs require our attention. God has chosen to use us to meet those needs. With His help and power, we can do it.

BELIEVERS ARE GIFTED TO MINISTER

Ministry has another dimension. It focuses on the work of believers in building up the church.

We cannot exclude meeting believers' needs from our definition of ministry. The goal of discipleship is the equipping of believers as ministers. Believers are gifted by the Holy Spirit to minister according to the will of God. The Holy Spirit is sovereign in dispensing gifts for ministry for the common good of the church (1 Cor. 12:7). Each believer is gifted by the Holy Spirit to fulfill a function in the church.

Ministry is not just the responsibility of professionally trained persons called ministers. Ministry is the normal function of every believer.

A church is a fellowship of believers redeemed by God out of sin and called by God out of the world to proclaim the gospel of Christ, to influence corrupt societies, and to build the kingdom of God. The responsibility each of us has is great and important. Our tasks and gifts

> Christian ministry needs God's blessings so that our efforts will result in meeting persons' needs and in winning the unsaved to Christ.

> The Holy Spirit is sovereign in dispensing gifts for ministry for the common good of the church.

will differ, but our working together to accomplish the Great Commission is the most important work in the world.

MINISTRY: A KINGDOM PRINCIPLE FOR CHURCH GROWTH

We cannot minister in isolation from others. When people speak of "my ministry," they reveal a dangerous misunderstanding of the nature of ministry. We do not own the ministry the Lord gives us. We are stewards of it. We cannot minister effectively without the power and giftedness of the Holy Spirit. Neither can we serve the Lord in the flesh.

The needs of churches and believers are constant and challenging. I cannot meet every need in my church by myself; but together with other believers and with the power of the Holy Spirit, we can meet the needs. The Lord will provide through His people and beyond His people the resources we need.

We make a mistake when we try to minister apart from the Holy Spirit's power and gifts. What a joy it is, though, to be a steward of the resources He provides.

The kingdom principle of ministry focuses on the church at work to meet the needs of those inside and outside its walls. No church can grow unless it commits to minister as the Lord provides need and opportunities.

5. WORSHIP (ACTS 2:46-47)

Worship is one of the most vital, if not the most vital, functions of the church. Worship that transforms is the response of believers to the presence, holiness, and revelation of Almighty God. Adoration of God and showing reverence for Him should be our first priority. We receive power, guidance, and spiritual strength when we genuinely worship.

Sometimes worship, as the Lord intended, gets lost in the glitz and glamour of churches trying to outdo one another by experimenting with different worship styles. That is not to say new approaches for worship are not to be considered. Indeed, they are. One approach will not meet all people's needs all the time. Paul stated:

We make a mistake when we try to minister apart from the aid of the Holy Spirit and other believers.

No church can grow unless it commits itself to minister.

Acts 2:46-47:

"And every day they devoted themselves to meeting together in the temple complex, and broke bread from house to house. They ate their food with gladness and simplicity of heart, praising God and having favor with all the people. And every day the Lord added those being saved to them" (Acts 2:46-47).

"I have become all things to all people, so that I may by all means save some" (1 Cor. 9:22).

However, we must be constantly alert to the importance in church growth of the essential elements of the kingdom principle of worship.

Rediscovery of Worship

This century marks the rediscovery and redefinition of worship in many churches. Life is changing at an accelerated rate, and so is church life. In churches across America, nothing is questioned, studied, and changed more than worship services. From the contemporary to the liturgical, believers are seeking forms of worship they enjoy and that give meaning to their Sundays.

Worship Is An Encounter with God

We must be alert to the essential elements of worship. Certainly, joy and meaning are to be sought in worship, but is that all there is to worship?

True worship is not form, whether traditional, liturgical, contemporary, or any combination of the three. Form very well may help people worship, but worship is any activity in which believers experience God in a meaningful, spiritually transforming way. True worship should lead worshipers to a deeper appreciation for God, a better understanding of His ways, and to a deeper commitment to Him. Encountering God in worship transforms us more and more into His likeness.

God Is the Object and Subject of Worship

God does not intend for worship to be an activity in which only believers' needs are met. Neither can worship be an event designed only for the needs of unbelievers. Worship must be designed to meet the needs of both.

Worship arises from the commands of God in Scripture and the grateful hearts of the redeemed, who long to come before the Lord to praise Him and to acknowledge His presence in their lives.

Worship is one of the most vital, if not the most vital, functions of the church.

Worship is any activity in which believers experience God in a meaningful, spiritually transforming way.

Worship arises from God's commands in Scripture and the grateful hearts of the redeemed.

GOD BEGINS AND CONTROLS WORSHIP

Worship begins with God, and not people; but it is for humanity's benefit, not God's. Worship is not something people do because they want to influence God. Worship is not something people do just out of gratitude, love, and fear. Emotions do not control worship; God controls worship. God instructs us how to worship and how not to worship.

The Books of Exodus, Leviticus, Numbers, and Deuteronomy gave Israel specific instructions about worship. God did not leave worship to the Israelites' imagination. He instructed them down to the smallest detail about how the tabernacle and ark of the covenant were to be built and handled and about their meaning. He even revealed with meticulous care how worship ceremonies were to be performed.

God is sovereign and holy. Worship must not be done according to our small notions of Him, our limited conceptions of what He wants, or what might please us. God is above all, and we are to worship Him in the manner He desires. We cannot lose this understanding without damaging our faithfulness to the Lord.

God is in charge of worship. He created us and redeems us at His pleasure. He gave forms of worship in the Old Testament to direct Israel's worship and has given His Holy Spirit in the New Testament to give us liberty and guidance in how to worship Him for who He is and what He has done.

LEADERS MATTER

For worship that transforms to occur, it must be guided by worship leaders who are believers, who have a kingdom focus, who understand the culture and context of the worshipers, who are themselves being transformed by the experience of worship, and who believe that God seeks those who worship Him in spirit and truth.

WORSHIPERS FIRST LISTEN TO GOD

We cannot allow ourselves to understand worship in terms of actions, orders of worship, forms, and music.

> Worship must not be done according to our small notions of God or what might please us.

> The Holy Spirit gives us liberty and guidance in how to worship God.

> We cannot allow ourselves to understand worship in terms of actions, orders of worship, forms (liturgy), and music.

Worship begins with God. We first listen to Him and what He says to do when we come into His presence.

Old Testament Worship

In the Old Testament, both in the tabernacle and in the temple, worship included the celebration of religious festivals, reverence for the ark of the covenant, sacrifices, and keeping the Sabbath. These experiences allowed Israel to reverence God and to rejoice in His provision as they remembered His everlasting covenant with them. Atonement for sins and recognition of a Holy God, who creates and redeems, were part of worship at the tabernacle and temple. Music was a prominent part of Israelite worship when Solomon built the temple.

Every part of Old Testament worship ritual was filled with meaning for those who participated. It expressed what God desired for His people.

New Testament Worship

In the New Testament, worship developed on the basis of a personal relationship with Christ and the indwelling of the Holy Spirit. The Spirit brings liberty and freedom to worship that were not present in Old Testament worshipers' experience (John 4:19-24).

The Spirit brings liberty and freedom to worship.

Eight Elements of New Testament Worship

The New Testament lists at least eight elements of worship the early church practiced. These elements serve as a pattern for us today. They are:

1. Prayer is communication with God that leads the congregation to an awareness of God's presence.— Jesus urged His followers not to pray like the hypocrites. He told His disciples to pray in secret, to pray without vain repetition, and to pray for God's kingdom to come. He also instructed them to pray for daily bread, for deliverance from temptation, for forgiveness, and for deliverance from evil, and to reverence God in all His power and glory as they prayed (Matt. 6:5-13).

Jesus reminded His many listeners during the Sermon on the Mount:

Eight elements of worship the early church practiced:

Prayer
Praise
Confession and Repentance
Confession of Faith
Scripture Reading and Study
Preaching
Lord's Supper and Baptism
Offerings

"But seek first the kingdom of God and His righteousness, and all these things will be provided for you" (Matt. 6:33).

Prayer was central in the early churches' worship. Paul urged the churches to pray for those in need, those having problems, the spread of the gospel, and for individuals who had sinned. The apostle encouraged the Thessalonians to:

"Pray constantly. Give thanks in everything, for this is God's will for you in Christ Jesus" (1 Thess. 5:17-18).

He urged the churches to pray for his missionary efforts and ministry. Paul wrote Timothy:

"Then, I urge that petitions, prayers, intercessions, and thanksgivings be made for everyone, for kings and all those who are in authority, so that we may lead a tranquil and quiet life in all godliness and dignity. This is good, and it pleases God our Savior" (1 Tim. 2:1-3).

2. Praise expresses to God our adoration and thanks for His character, being, and work, and assists the congregation in understanding the reality of God's kingdom and His reign over the world and their lives.
— Praise was a major element in the early churches' worship (Acts 2:46-47). Paul and Silas conducted a worship service when they were imprisoned in Philippi for preaching the gospel.

"About midnight Paul and Silas were praying and singing hymns to God, and the prisoners were listening to them" (Acts 16:25).

God's people often expressed His praise in songs and hymns. Throughout the Old Testament, the Israelites praised God in songs for their deliverance, for His miracles, for His intervention in their lives. Early believers praised Jesus in songs for what He had done for them (Eph. 5:19; Col. 3:16).

Paul charged the believers in Rome:

Prayer was central in the early churches' worship.

Praise was a major element in the early churches' worship.

"And so that Gentiles may glorify God for His mercy. As it is written: 'Therefore I will praise You among the Gentiles, and I will sing psalms to Your name'. Again it says: 'Rejoice, you Gentiles, with His people!' And again: 'Praise the Lord, all you Gentiles; all the peoples should praise Him!'" (Rom. 15:9-11).

Praise must be a major element in our churches today. We praise the Lord for creating us and for redeeming us in Christ. God's praise is not just an emotional outburst from our hearts. We come before the Lord to praise Him because He has directed us in His Word to do so. Moses declared:

"He is thy praise, and he is thy God, that hath done for thee these great and terrible things, which thine eyes have seen" (Deut. 10:21).

We do not praise God simply because He has blessed us and has done good things for us. We praise Him because He wants us to praise Him and because He commands us to do so.

Praise is not driven so much by our feelings as by our obedience. Worship can be boring only when we are the center of it and do not focus on God.

3. Confession and Repentance. — God restores fellowship when the congregation confesses (agrees with God regarding the reality of their sin) and repents (turns from their sin to God). Confession is at the heart of worship, which pleases our Lord. Worship is a time to allow the Lord to change our minds, hearts, and lives, and a time to dedicate ourselves to Him.

We are not to listen passively to music, prayers, and sermons in worship services and not be affected and changed by the worship experience. After we experience the presence of the Lord in worship, we cannot be the same. We are apt to see our own sinfulness and shortcomings in the presence of a holy God and cry out in confession of our sins and our weaknesses.

Worship is a time to hear from the Lord and be changed by His presence, power, and Word.

> Praise is not driven so much by our feelings as by our obedience.

4. Confession of faith in God the Father, Son, and Holy Spirit. Profession provides the opportunity for the congregation to acknowledge and respond to God's Word and His activity. — Paul wrote the believers in Rome:

> *"If you confess with your mouth, 'Jesus is Lord,' and believe in your heart that God raised Him from the dead, you will be saved. With the heart one believes, resulting in righteousness, and with the mouth one confesses, resulting in salvation" (Rom. 10:9-10).*

When we confess our faith in the Father, Son, and Holy Spirit, we declare that God alone is Creator, Redeemer, and Sustainer. We declare that He alone is worthy to receive glory and honor and praise.

5. Scripture reading and study. Since God transforms the congregation through His Word, worship includes substantial portions of Scripture. — Hearing, reading, and studying Scripture are essential to a healthy Christian life. The Holy Spirit uses reading, hearing, and studying Scripture to draw our attention to God and to our fellowship with Him.

Scripture was important to Jesus (Luke 4:16-21). After His resurrection, He appeared to two of His disciples on the road to Emmaus. The two disciples did not know they were talking to the risen Lord. When Jesus questioned them about their sad looks, they related to Him the events of the crucifixion and burial and expressed their doubts about His resurrection. Jesus reproved them for their unbelief and taught them the truth from the Scriptures.

> *"Then beginning with Moses and all the Prophets, He interpreted for them in all the Scriptures the things concerning Himself" (Luke 24:27).*

After these disciples recognized Jesus, He vanished and appeared later to His disciples in Jerusalem (Luke 24:31, 36-43). The two disciples were amazed at what they had witnessed and said to each other:

Worship is a time to hear from the Lord and be changed by His presence, power, and Word.

Reading and studying the Scriptures are crucial in our worship.

"Weren't our hearts ablaze within us while He was talking with us on the road and explaining the Scriptures to us?" (Luke 24:32).

Jesus demonstrated to His disciples gathered in Jerusalem that He had risen from the dead by showing them His pierced hands and feet. He opened to them the Scriptures and explained how they were fulfilled in Him.

"Then He told them, 'These are My words that I spoke to you while I was still with you, that everything written about Me in the Law of Moses, the Prophets, and the Psalms must be fulfilled.' Then He opened their minds to understand the Scriptures" (Luke 24:44-45).

Reading and studying the Scriptures were a significant part of the early church's worship (1 Tim. 4:13). These activities are no less crucial in our worship today.

6. Preaching. God uses the preaching of His Word to instruct, teach, challenge, confront, convict, and exhort the congregation to obey His Word. — Preaching is central in worship services, because it focuses on the Lord and His magnificence. The church is to proclaim His Word and His person, power, and name within and without its walls. His truth, nature, and message are to be proclaimed everywhere by every believer. God's people are to hear from His Word the things of God. The proclamation of the Word of God evangelizes, edifies, and educates. Nothing can substitute for preaching in the church's worship services. Preaching speaks God's truth to His people and prepares them to be His messengers.

Paul wrote believers in Rome:

"Therefore, brothers, by the mercies of God, I urge you to present your bodies as a living sacrifice, holy and pleasing to God; this is your spiritual worship. Do not be conformed to this age, but be transformed by the renewing of your mind, so that you may discern what is the good, pleasing, and perfect will of God" (Rom. 12:1-2).

The Holy Spirit uses reading, hearing, and studying Scripture to draw our attention to God.

Preaching is central to worship.

The proclamation of the Word of God evangelizes, edifies, and educates.

63

KINGDOM PRINCIPLES FOR CHURCH GROWTH

Paul referred to the sacrifice of our lives as our "spiritual worship" to the Lord. When we worship the Lord, we come before Him in prayer, confession, and praise, to hear His Word.

7. Lord's Supper and Baptism. Jesus established the ordinances as dramatic symbols to make the congregation aware of His work on their behalf. — The Lord's Supper and baptism are two beautiful, moving acts of worship Jesus gave us to remember Him by.

We can easily imagine how poignant the moments were when Jesus gave the broken bread to His disciples just hours before He was crucified. He looked into the eyes of those disciples whom He would assign to go into all the world and said those never-to-be-forgotten words: "Do this in remembrance of Me." Then he took the cup and said, "This cup is the new covenant in My blood, which is shed for you" (Luke 22:19-20).

Jesus' request to be baptized took John by surprise. John declared: "I need to be baptized by You, and yet You come to me?" (Matt. 3:14). Jesus urged John to baptize Him. Jesus declared that it was appropriate for Him to be baptized to fulfill all righteousness. The Scriptures declare:

"After Jesus was baptized, He went up immediately from the water. The heavens suddenly opened for Him, and He saw the Spirit of God descending like a dove and coming down on Him. And there came a voice from heaven: This is My beloved Son. I take delight in Him!" (Matt. 3:16-17).

Believers are to follow Jesus' example, and churches are to make baptism a crucial part of their worship. Jesus' disciples, the early church, and early missionaries incorporated baptism into their worship. On the day of Pentecost, those who heard Peter's message asked him and the rest of the apostles what they must do. " 'Repent,' Peter said to them, 'and be baptized, each of you, in the name of Jesus the Messiah for the forgiveness of your sins, and you will receive the gift of the Holy Spirit'" (Acts 2:37-38).

The Lord's Supper and baptism are two beautiful, moving acts of worship.

Churches are to make baptism a crucial part of their worship.

64

"So those who accepted his message were baptized, and that day about three thousand people were added to them" (Acts 2:41).

Paul emphasized the importance of baptism:

"There is one body and one Spirit, just as you were called to one hope at your calling; one Lord, one faith, one baptism, one God and Father of all, who is above all and through all and in all" (Eph. 4:4-6).

8. *Offerings. Giving of self, abilities, and tithes and offerings to God are responses of obedient stewardship, gratitude, and trust.* — Worship requires the giving of ourselves in obedience to God. Our lives are to be our first offering to our Lord.

Paul mentioned giving ourselves in Romans 12:1-2. We are to present our bodies a living sacrifice, holy, acceptable to God, which is our reasonable service.

We also are to give of our means. Giving is an act of worship, of recognition of what our Lord has done for us. In his final instructions to the church at Philippi, Paul gave thanks for their generosity.

Our lives are to be our first offering to our Lord.

"And you, Philippians, know that in the early days of the gospel, when I left Macedonia, no church shared with me in the matter of giving and receiving except you alone. For even in Thessalonica you sent gifts for my need several times. Not that I seek the gift: but I seek the fruit that is increasing to your account. . . . And my God will supply all your needs according to His riches in glory in Christ Jesus" (Phil. 4:15-17, 19).

Giving is an act of worship.

65

ELEMENTS ARE MORE IMPORTANT THAN METHODS

The order of these eight elements of worship in the early churches is not established in the Scriptures. Each seems to have had a vital place in the early New Testament churches. Believers and churches have the freedom to worship the Father as they are led by the Holy Spirit.

The forms of worship are as many as the cultures in which the Lord is worshiped, but the elements of worship are consistent throughout the New Testament. The subject and object of worship is God: Father, Son, and Holy Spirit.

THE PURPOSE OF OUR WORSHIP

The purpose of worship is to come before the Lord in obedience to praise Him, to hear from Him, to confess to Him, and to commit our lives to Him. Every worship service is to be an encounter with the Lord, transcending our feelings, desires, and even our abilities to perform. Worship calls for individuals to respond. Whether this response is shared with others present or is a private response of the heart, it leads to lifestyle change.

PERSONAL AND FAMILY WORSHIP ARE VITAL

In addition to corporate worship, every church needs to teach its members the value of personal and family worship. A church family is a fellowship bound together for more than one day a week.

In reality, the church is a fellowship scattered throughout the community until it gathers in a place for worship and Bible study. Worship is to be marked by prayer, praise, Scripture reading, and instruction.

While we need to gather in our places of worship on the Lord's day and on other days, we have the Holy Spirit to guide and to lead us in worship any place, any time. We are to obey the biblical admonition to worship the Lord corporately, in our families, and in our personal walk with the Lord.

> Believers and churches have the freedom to worship the Father as they are led by the Holy Spirit.

> Every worship service is to be an encounter with the Lord.

FIVE THINGS EACH CHURCH MUST DO TO GROW

To summarize, we have:

1 driving force of church growth:
    The Great Commission

5 essential church functions for church growth:
    Evangelism
    Discipleship
    Fellowship
    Ministry
    Worship

And now, the *4* results.

We have the Holy Spirit to guide and to lead us in worship any place, any time.

If we do these *five* functions, we will experience the *four* results discussed in chapter 4.

FOUR RESULTS OF KINGDOM GROWTH

J esus declared: *"But seek first the kingdom of God and His righteousness, and all these things will be provided for you" (Matt. 6:33).*

As we evangelize, disciple, fellowship, minister, and worship, we must never forget that we are seeking God's kingdom and its growth. However, keeping our perspective right is difficult when so many pressing issues and problems impact us in our church work. Completing the kingdom is the goal of God's activity in our world, and our task is to do whatever it takes to share with Him in growing His kingdom. All of the effort we invest in growing churches must result in increasing God's kingdom.

Seeking God's kingdom is our first priority. — When God's kingdom is our first priority and guide, church growth takes its proper place in the work, planning, and service we do. Church growth is an outgrowth of doing kingdom work well.

The nature of church growth has been defined in many ways in recent years. Discussions of the methods and meaning of church growth are greater now than at any time in recent history. We have more resources promising to help churches grow than ever before. We have private institutes, seminary centers, and denominational organizations studying and promoting church growth. A vast array of conferences, resources, workshops, consultants, and teaching-churches have sprung up across the world. This emphasis on church growth is a positive sign and needed by all churches. Still, we need to give attention to more than methods, models, and techniques. We need to focus on the dynamics for church growth provided by the kingdom of God if we expect to see enduring results.

Church growth is not the result of methods. — True church growth is not the result of methods. It is the result of the supernatural activity of God, who desires to redeem persons to Himself. When a church discovers and applies the kingdom principles of church growth, increases in the church naturally follow.

> True church growth is the outcome of God's supernatural activity.

Many people associate church growth only with numerical increase. That idea is too limited. Churches move in life-cycles or stages. These include birth, development, growth, plateau, decline, and sometimes death. In spite of the rise and fall in church growth, the kingdom of God never stops growing. Churches are living agents of kingdom growth; but not every church can, does, or will grow numerically forever. The kingdom of God always is growing numerically, but individual churches may or may not increase.

> The kingdom of God always is growing numerically, but individual churches may or may not increase.

Church growth is not measured only by numbers.—Four kinds of growth result when a body of believers faithfully follows the essential functions of kingdom growth. Evangelism, discipleship, ministry, fellowship, and worship, when applied to fulfilling the Great Commission, result in church growth in four dimensions: numerical, spiritual transformation, ministry expansion, and kingdom advance.

> Church growth should not and cannot be measured only in terms of numerical growth.

1. Numerical Growth

Numerical growth means the numerical increase of the church measured in membership, in baptisms, and in attendance levels. Since the kingdom of God is increasing numerically, churches that practice the kingdom principles of evangelism, discipleship, ministry, fellowship, and worship grow numerically. When we do these things in the power of God, we gather a harvest of souls. A harvest means God, through the witness of believers, adds numbers to the body of Christ. When persons accept Jesus Christ by faith, they are brought from death to life and welcomed into the body of Christ. Each second, someone, somewhere, is saved by God's grace and brought into the kingdom.

Everyone Needs to Hear the Gospel

Some persons discount the value of numerical growth in favor of spiritual growth. Neither should be discounted. Both are important. God is at work guiding believers in their spiritual growth. As believers grow spiritually, God gives the churches numerical increase. Both numerical and spiritual growth are God's work. To fail to expect the increases God gives is to doubt God.

God sends us into the world to preach and teach the gospel to persons He has created and longs to redeem. He wants us to have a strong desire to reach them with the good news of salvation in Christ.

The need for redemption is universal. Our task is to take the message of redemption to all people throughout the world.

Importance of Numbers

Without a proper view of the Great Commission, we can lose sight of the significance of numbers. Numbers outside and inside the body of Christ are indicators of what is happening in church and kingdom growth. Those who need the Lord and those who know Him are counted. Numerical increase in the church follows true kingdom service.

Jesus declared His intention to build His church on believers' profession of faith and discipleship when He said to Peter:

"And I also say to you that you are Peter, and on this rock I will build My church, and the forces of Hades will not overpower it" (Matt. 16:18).

The reports of the first-century churches clearly reveal that God was at work among them. Notice how naturally the Scriptures mention numbers:

"So those who accepted his message were baptized, and that day about three thousand people were added to them" (Acts 2:41).

"But many of those who heard the message believed, and the number of the men came to about five thousand" (Acts 4:4).

> As believers grow spiritually, God gives the churches numerical increase.

> Numbers outside and inside the body of Christ are indicators of what is happening in church and kingdom growth.

"So the preaching about God flourished, the number of the disciples in Jerusalem multiplied greatly, and a large group of priests became obedient to the faith" (Acts 6:7).

"The Lord's hand was with them, and a large number who believed turned to the Lord" (Acts 11:21).

Numbers Indicate God Is at Work

The danger is not in using numbers to see what God is doing. It is in seeing numbers as statistics rather than as people and in using them as the sole measure of church growth rather than as indicators of God's activity in the churches and in His kingdom.

Statistics are recorded in Scripture to reveal the number of lives touched by God's power and changed forever by His grace. Statistics can be used for many purposes; but rarely do they, by themselves, prove anything conclusively. However, numbers do indicate that the kingdom of God is increasing constantly in the world.

Numbers Are Not to Be Discounted

If we discount the value of numerical growth, several dangers confront us. We will have less and less motivation to evangelize our family, friends, neighbors, and other lost persons we meet. We will have less motivation to join God in His mission of redeeming a people to Himself. We will lose sight of the Bible's message that the time persons have to be saved from their sins and the time we have to reach them with the gospel is limited.

Peter said of the time and opportunities we have:

"The Lord does not delay His promise, as some understand delay, but is patient with you, not wanting any to perish, but all to come to repentance" (2 Pet. 3:9).

The numbers in attendance, baptism, and ministry participation records indicate whether our efforts in the church are following God's pattern and will. Numerical increases reveal some of the results of God's work around us and through us to save persons.

> The problem is in seeing numbers as statistics rather than as people and in using them as the sole measure of church growth.

> If we discount the value of numerical growth, we will have less motivation to evangelize our friends, neighbors, and other lost persons we meet.

71

Second, we risk losing touch with the heart of God if we discount the value of numbers. God's heart is set on reaching out to persons wherever they are and in whatever condition they live. He longs to redeem them, to change their lives, and to care for them. He wants people to live abundantly and to reach their highest potential.

Numerical Growth Brings New Life and Hope

If we discount numerical growth in the body of Christ, we lose sight of people who need the Lord.

The Father has determined the very moment when Christ will return to earth to take His people to their heavenly home. He has not revealed the time; but we must conclude with Peter that this time of waiting means the Lord wants more people to enter the kingdom.

Numerical growth brings new life and hope into the church and reminds us to be about our Father's business.

We Can Be Assured of Numerical Growth

God wants more people saved, and we can be sure that He will give the increase if we practice the five kingdom principles of church growth. More people live in our world than ever before. Therefore, we have the potential for more persons to be saved than ever before.

Our task is to fulfill the five essential functions of church growth in order to enjoy numerical growth. We are surrounded by lost persons. The kingdom of God is growing. The Father, Son, and Holy Spirit are working in the world to redeem persons. When our efforts are guided by our Lord, we can be sure that our churches will experience numerical growth.

2. SPIRITUAL TRANSFORMATION

Practicing the principles of kingdom growth also results in spiritual transformation. The Scriptures lay heavy emphasis on spiritual transformation. It is one of the fundamental requirements Christ gave in the Great Commission when He said we were to be:

God's heart is set on reaching out to persons wherever they are and in whatever condition they live.

We can be sure that God will give the increase if we practice the five kingdom principles of church growth.

"Teaching them to observe everything I have commanded you."

If numerical growth is all a church strives for, the outcome will be the creation of something "a mile wide and a half-inch deep." Our Lord does not intend for kingdom growth to be shallow. Kingdom growth assuredly involves numerical growth; but for the continued growth of believers and the expansion of the kingdom, much more is involved. The Lord commanded us to reach out to people in His power. He promised to redeem people and to transform them into His disciples. Spiritual transformation is God's work of changing a believer into the likeness of Jesus by creating a new identity in Christ and by empowering a lifelong relationship of love, trust, and obedience to glorify God (2 Cor. 3:18).

> He promised to redeem people and to transform them into His disciples.

Disciples Are to Grow in Spiritual Maturity

We are not finished products. We have not reached the end of our journey, but we are on our way (Phil. 3:13-14). Paul refers to believers in Galatia as "my children" (Gal. 4:19).

The analogies of children and a new birth in Christ are exceedingly appropriate. Born-again persons need to learn, to understand, to practice, and to model the meaning of being a disciple of our Lord and Savior. Day by day, year by year, children pass through stages of growth on the way to maturity; so do believers. Newborn Christians are expected to grow spiritually just as newborn children are expected to grow.

And just as small children need help and encouragement to talk, walk, and ultimately become responsible adults, new Christians need the support and guidance of the church to grow and to mature spiritually. Peter urged all believers to:

> New Christians need the support and guidance of the church to mature spiritually.

"Grow in the grace and knowledge of our Lord and Savior Jesus Christ. To Him be the glory both now and to the day of eternity. Amen" (2 Pet. 3:18)

Stages of Spiritual Transformation

Disciples are at various stages of spiritual maturity. Some are babes in Christ. Some are growing and struggling to become like Him. Others are spiritually mature. Some, unfortunately, are doing little or nothing to grow in Christ.

Jesus commanded us to make disciples. He also demonstrated in His life what the life of a disciple is like. He modeled the abundant, Spirit-controlled life, and He taught us how to live it. His example of spiritually mature living is the type of life He urges believers to model. As the example of Christ is lived out in the fellowship of the church, spiritual transformation takes place.

Spiritual transformation is addressed abundantly throughout the Scriptures. Moses admonished the Israelites to love the Lord their God with all their heart, soul, and might (Deut. 6:4-5). Then in words that should leave no doubt in anyone's mind that God's Word must be taught to His children so they can live pleasing to Him, Moses said:

"And thou shalt teach them diligently unto thy children, and shalt talk of them when thou sittest in thine house, and when thou walkest by the way, and when thou liest down, and when thou risest up" (Deut. 6:7).

The church must be busy at the task of teaching if believers are to be spiritually transformed.

The Gift of Eternal Life and Forgiveness

God's free gift of life through faith in Christ has two important dimensions all believers share and enjoy. The first is eternal life.

"For God loved the world in this way: He gave His only Son, so that everyone who believes in Him will not perish but have eternal life" (John 3:16).

The second great benefit that comes to us the moment we believe in Christ is the forgiveness of our sins.

Jesus' example of spiritually mature living is the type of life He urges believers to model.

As the example of Christ is lived out in the fellowship of the church, spiritual growth takes place.

We are delivered from the guilt and penalty of sin and are brought into a right relationship with God. Peter declared:

"For Christ also suffered for sins once for all, the righteous for the unrighteous, that He might bring you to God, after being put to death in the fleshly realm but made alive in the spiritual realm" (1 Pet. 3:18).

Spiritual Transformation Begins at Conversion

The gift of eternal life and forgiveness is the beginning of the Christian life. Eternal life is a present possession for every believer the moment he or she trusts Christ as Savior; but salvation continues from conversion, to spiritual maturity, through the resurrection, and into all eternity.

When God saves individuals and brings them into His eternal kingdom, He longs for them to become more and more like Him. He wants them to grow in the grace and knowledge of our Lord Jesus Christ. Paul said becoming a Christian is a transforming experience that radically changes us from what we were to what Jesus Christ wants us to be.

"And you were dead in your trespasses and sins" (Eph. 2:1).

"We all, with unveiled faces, are reflecting the glory of the Lord and are being transformed into the same image from glory to glory" (2 Cor. 3:18).

The Abundant Life in Christ

The beginning of the Christian life never will be repeated. We have no desire or need to go back to what we were. Our next step is to go on to the mature Christian life the Father intends. Jesus referred to this in John 10:10 as the abundant life.

"I have come that they may have life and have it in abundance."

Salvation continues from conversion, to spiritual maturity, through the resurrection, and into all eternity.

Spiritual transformation is a lifelong process that goes beyond knowledge to dynamic Christian living.

Paul, the missionary-evangelist of the first century, struck the note of spiritual maturity when he declared:

"We proclaim Him, warning and teaching everyone with all wisdom, so that we may present everyone mature in Christ" (Col. 1:28).

He also stated the same spiritual growth principle to the believers in Ephesus:

"And He personally gave some to be apostles, some prophets, some evangelists, some pastors and teachers, for the training of the saints in the work of ministry, to build up the body of Christ" (Eph. 4:11-12).

Spiritual Transformation's Four Dimensions

The spiritual maturity of believers is a goal and mark of a growing church. The growth of God's kingdom is measured not only by numerical growth, it also is measured by believers' spiritual transformation in at least four dimensions:

1. Developing in our relationship with Christ. — First, we must develop in our relationship with Christ. Our fellowship and intimacy with the Lord are essential to spiritual transformation. Growth in Christ is more than growth in knowledge and experience. Transformation is growth in Christlikeness — not an option for believers; it is a requirement. Jesus said:

"I am the vine; you are the branches. The one who remains in Me and I in him produces much fruit, because you can do nothing without Me" (John 15:5).

Christ's words are plain. Make no mistake: We get our daily growth and spiritual nourishment from the same source we get eternal life — Jesus Christ.

Our relationship with Christ is the most important matter in our lives. We do not live daily on our own strength and only go to Christ when we urgently need

> The growth of God's kingdom is measured not only by numerical growth, it also is measured by believers' spiritual transformation.

> Our fellowship and intimacy with the Lord are essential to spiritual transformation.

help, comfort, and guidance. The abundant life does not exist apart from constant fellowship with Him.

God invites us to enter a love relationship with Him. He does not invite us to be saved through the blood of Christ and go our own way apart from Him.

Jesus longs for us to have the same kind of relationship with Him that He has with the Father. The Savior prayed this tender prayer for us just a few hours before His death:

"May they all be one, just as You, Father, are in Me and I am in You. May they also be one in Us, so that the world may believe You sent Me" (John 17:21).

We are to grow in our relationships with Him to the point that He lives His life in and through us. Paul expressed this when he wrote:

"I have been crucified with Christ; and I no longer live, but Christ lives in me. The life I now live in the flesh, I live by faith in the Son of God, who loved me and gave Himself for me" (Gal. 2:19-20).

Paul's life was transformed dramatically by God's grace when he placed his faith in Christ. After Paul met Christ on the road to Damascus, he no longer could live his old life. He was a new man; Christ now lived in him. We also must grow in our relationship with Christ until we:

"Set your minds on what is above, not on what is on the earth. For you have died, and your life is hidden with the Messiah in God. When the Messiah, who is your life, is revealed, then you also will be revealed with Him in glory" (Col. 3:2-4).

2. Developing in our relationships with believers. — Second, we must grow in our relationships with other believers. The mark of a growing church is the warm, loving relationships believers enjoy with one another. God creates each of us in His image, but no two persons are alike. We are different, with many different backgrounds, cultures, ideas, opinions, and experiences. We do not

> We are to grow in our relationships with Christ to the point that He lives His life in and through us.

> The mark of a growing church is the warm, loving relationships believers enjoy with one another.

agree on many things, but each of us is a part of God's family. Galatians 3:26-28 declares:

> "For you are all sons of God through faith in Christ Jesus. For as many of you as have been baptized into Christ have put on Christ. There is no Jew or Greek, slave or free, male or female; for you are all one in Christ Jesus."

These verses speak to our position with one another in Christ. We are equal before God, but we are different in gender, personality, responsibility, and in a host of other ways. Even so, being one with Christ means we are one with one another. The Holy Spirit has many roles in our lives and in church growth, but none are more important than to provide unity in the bond of love.

Growing churches grow believers in a deeper relationship with Christ and with other believers. Walking in unity with other Christians is not difficult when the Holy Spirit controls our lives, minds, tongues, and actions. When we allow Christ to live His life through us and to express Himself in what we say, think, and do, we have no trouble being in fellowship with one another.

Spiritual transformation in a church builds the fellowship of believers into a family of Christian men, women, young persons, and children that sustains them in the most difficult times and circumstances. John said:

> "Love consists in this: not that we loved God, but that He loved us and sent His Son to be the propitiation for our sins. Dear friends, if God loved us in this way, we also must love one another" (1 John 4:10-11).

Our salvation is expressed in our love for Christ and for fellow believers in the family of God.

3. Developing relationships with the unsaved. — The third dimension of spiritual transformation in believers' lives is in relationship to those who are separated from God. Those who are lost are objects of the Father's love and concern and must be on our hearts and minds as well.

Walking in unity with other Christians is not difficult when the Holy Spirit controls our lives, minds, tongues and actions.

Those who are lost are objects of the Father's love and concern and must be on our hearts and minds as well.

True disciples of Christ grow in their relationship to God and other believers, but they also have a deep desire to see others saved. Jesus' disciples have a passion to see others saved and brought into a love-relationship with Him. It cannot be otherwise, for the Scriptures say:

"Now everything is from God, who reconciled us to Himself through Christ and gave us the ministry of reconciliation" (2 Cor. 5:18).

"But you will receive power when the Holy Spirit has come upon you, and you will be My witnesses in Jerusalem, in all Judea and Samaria, and to the ends of the earth" (Acts 1:8).

"But as for you, keep a clear head about everything, endure hardship, do the work of an evangelist, fulfill your ministry" (2 Tim. 4:5).

We never can separate discipleship from evangelism in our lives and churches. In a real sense, they are one and the same. We are to stay in constant contact with unbelievers in order to witness to them and to win them to Christ. God has no other plan for world redemption than to use each of us to win others to Christ. Spiritual transformation in a church results in believers learning their responsibility to witness to the lost.

4. Developing Christian discipline. — The fourth dimension of spiritual transformation is Christian discipline. The Christian life is built on such important disciplines as Bible reading and study, prayer, worship, witnessing, and faithful participation in the fellowship of believers. Discipleship, built on these disciplines, must be modeled and taught to believers in the body of Christ.

These activities will not of themselves produce mature Christians, but believers in Christ need the benefit of these activities to grow in spiritual maturity.

Every believer must be encouraged and trained to follow his or her heartfelt desire to know the Lord in a deeper relationship and to grow in love toward other

We cannot be Jesus' disciples and not have a passion to see others saved.

We never can separate discipleship from evangelism in our lives and churches.

Christians. Church growth is not possible without instructing believers in the Bible, in doctrine, and in Christian living and thinking.

Growing churches nurture their members by teaching and leading them to practice Christian disciplines so that they may grow in the grace and knowledge of our Lord. A church that practices the five essential functions of church growth will experience the right kind of spiritual transformation.

3. MINISTRY EXPANSION

The third result of church growth is expansion of ministry in the body of Christ. Young, developing churches usually are busy with basic structural ministries. They must build foundation ministries such as Sunday School and worship, which minister to believers and unbelievers. When Bible study and worship are established, other needs surface; and ministries are added to meet those needs. Growing churches discover that as they grow numerically and spiritually, the Holy Spirit opens additional doors of ministry to them through the lives of growing believers.

As churches experience the power of God working in unbelievers to bring them to Christ and in believers to grow them spiritually, they become more sensitive to needs in the fellowship, the community, and the world. They become more aware of the need to expand their ministry.

Churches that practice kingdom principles of growth will be amazed at how naturally the members seek out areas of ministry in which to serve.

Believers are gifted to minister. — Every believer in the body of Christ is gifted for specific service. The Holy Spirit determines who gets what gifts for ministries needed by the church. Paul wrote:

"Now there are different gifts, but the same Spirit. . . . But one and the same Spirit is active in all these, distributing to each one as He wills" (1 Cor. 12:4,11).

> Growing churches discover that as they grow numerically and spiritually, the Holy Spirit opens additional doors of ministry to them through the lives of growing believers.

> Every believer in the body of Christ is gifted for specific service.

As the body of Christ matures and grows, the Holy Spirit raises up needs and opportunities for ministry as well as gifted believers to meet those needs.

The needs of the world are greater today than at anytime in history. The resources to meet those needs are more critical than ever before. How can churches show the love and care of Christ to persons in our communities and around the world?

To ignore persons who hurt and go hungry never entered God's mind. He plans to meet those needs through the lives of His children He has placed around the world. Remember Jesus' words:

"When did we see You hungry and feed You, or thirsty and give You something to drink? When did we see You a stranger and take You in, or without clothes and clothe You? When did we see You sick, or in prison, and visit You? And the King will answer them, 'I assure you: Whatever you did for one of the least of these brothers of Mine, you did for Me.'" (Matt. 25:37-40).

"For even the Son of Man did not come to be served, but to serve, and to give His life — a ransom for many" (Mark 10:45).

Empowered to minister. — The Lord does not expect us to meet all the needs of all persons around the world in our own power. He would not place us under that kind of burden. We do not have the plan, resources, or ability to meet needs of that magnitude. However, we are not passive in this situation. God expects us to place our resources and abilities in His hands for His use. He will bless them, multiply them, and add to them so that we will have more than enough to meet the needs of all people. When we yield ourselves and our possessions fully to God and follow His leadership, we can minister in His name to anyone, anywhere in the world.

God empowers us to minister with His resources according to His will. He allows us to be channels of mercy and ministry to others. The Holy Spirit touches the lives of believers to show them the needs of humanity, across

> The Holy Spirit raises up needs and opportunities for ministry as well as gifted believers to meet those needs.

> The Lord does not expect us to meet all the needs of all persons around the world in our own power. He expects us to place our resources and abilities in His hands for His use.

the street and across the world. He wants us to bear the burden of love He has for those persons and to minister to them.

How can we meet people's needs when we do not have adequate resources? That question may grow out of our lack of faith and our acting like the things we have are ours, not His. We are not owners; we are stewards in the kingdom of God. We minister with His resources to people according to His leadership and will. The Holy Spirit gifts and equips us as ministers and stewards of the things of God, to be used and multiplied in the lives of people in need.

Growing churches expand their ministry. — Growing churches produce stewards who expand the churches' ministry under the Holy Spirit's leadership. When the body of Christ is growing numerically and spiritually, the Lord moves in the hearts and lives of people to do wonderful things. Extraordinary things happen, and the needs of people are met in unusual ways.

David said it well when he wrote:

Extraordinary things happen, and the needs of people are met in unusual ways when churches are growing.

"The earth is the Lord's, and the fulness thereof; the world, and they that dwell therein" (Ps. 24:1).

John pointed out the power and authority believers have in Christ:

"I assure you: The one who believes in Me will also do the works that I do. And he will do even greater works than these, because I am going to the Father" (John 14:12).

Since the Lord created all things, He has the resources to do what He wishes through His people. He wants to provide us with His fullness. We are to take what He gives us and go where He sends us to minister to those who need us. As we go, we can be sure that, in God's power, we can accomplish the work He has given us to do.

If churches forget they are in kingdom service, their ministries will be nothing more than those of secular benevolent and charitable organizations.

Each believer is called to kingdom service and is a steward of the kingdom. Each church is called out for kingdom service. If, however, believers and churches forget they are in kingdom service, their ministry will become just useful programs and benevolent activities that take the time and energy of God's people. Such ministry will be nothing more than those of secular benevolent and charitable organizations.

The Holy Spirit directs us to ministry. — If the strategies and plans we develop in our churches are only our plans and strategies, we lose sight of our kingdom stewardship. We also lose the power, presence, and freshness of the Holy Spirit to direct us according to God's will and in the ministry He chooses for us.

Nothing is wrong with programs, ministries, and activities in churches. However, they may or may not be the will of God for a particular church at a particular time unless the church has sought and found God's will in the endeavors in which it wishes to engage.

Every church must have ministries of evangelism, discipleship, ministry, fellowship, and worship to be obedient to God. Believers are to bathe each ministry in prayer and promote it aggressively. But the Spirit of God must guide believers and churches to do what He desires.

God is at work bringing people into His kingdom in this world and preparing them to abide in His eternal presence in the next. We must find out from the Lord what He wants us to do in ministry.

Listen to the Holy Spirit. — A growing church listens to the Holy Spirit's voice through the Word of God and prayer and depends on the Spirit to lead it to the ministry He desires.

Often the Lord leads a church to do things in ministry that are unusual and out of the church's normal pattern. The more mature believers are, the more likely God will lead them to do greater and different things.

In the parable of the talents, Jesus spoke of the servants' faithfulness to the responsibility the master had given them. This resulted in the master giving them greater service responsibilities.

"For to everyone who has, more will be given, and he will have more than enough. But from the one who does not

> If the strategies and plans we develop are only our plans and strategies, we lose sight of our kingdom stewardship.

> The more mature believers are, the more likely God will lead them to do greater and different things.

have, even what he has will be taken away from him" (Matt. 25:29).

God has much more for believers than they have ever imagined. — Paul wrote about the wonderful way God reveals Himself, His will, and His vast store of treasures to us:

"But as it is written: What no eye has seen and no ear has heard, and what has never come into a man's heart, is what God has prepared for those who love Him. Now God has revealed them to us by the Spirit, for the Spirit searches everything, even the deep things of God" (1 Cor. 2:9-10).

God cannot be fully understood, can never be predicted, and is not bound to work according to our expectations and plans. He chooses to do things His way for His purposes, which include His calling, equipping, and empowering His children to do many wonderful things.

A growing church will enjoy the freshness of the Lord's raising up believers to do ministry beyond the ordinary. As ministry is expanded, the freshness in the body of Christ reveals that the kingdom is growing.

Expanding ministry reveals that the kingdom of God is growing.

4. KINGDOM ADVANCE

The logical order of the results of growing churches and believers practicing the five essential kingdom principles moves from numerical and spiritual growth to ministry and kingdom advance. This is the Great Commission enacted in its purest and best form. Remember, however, the Great Commission's "go" is not complete until people are sent out from local churches — to advance His kingdom — as the Lord directs.

The Great Commission's "go" is not complete until people are sent out from local churches as the Lord directs.

Growing churches practice missions. — Each person must be reached with the gospel. When that person is redeemed, he or she must be discipled and equipped to live for Christ and to serve Him. Believers, gifted for ministry, serve the Lord as He directs.

A church is not growing as it should if it increases numerically, develops spiritually, and expands its ministry, but does not involve itself in missions. The final element of church growth is involvement and commitment to kingdom advance through missions.

Although the results of church growth cannot be separated from one another, missions are the piece that puts the work of the church into proper perspective. Missions are the crown of a church's ministry. It reveals that the people of God have developed a worldview that is proper and biblical.

God has one strategy for all nations. — God does not have one strategy to save people in one nation and another to save people in a different nation. He does not view persons in Asia differently from those in Europe. He has not blessed North America and punished South America. Jesus Christ came into the world to save every person in the world. We have one Lord and one way of salvation. We have one message to preach and one call to repentance and faith. God has one kingdom and one church, but He has many local churches who are to be on mission with Him.

Let's review some basic truths about believers. These will help us understand the important role of all believers in kingdom advance:

- Every believer is a minister. We all are saved for service in God's kingdom.

- Every believer is called of God to minister. Some are trained pastors and staff persons in churches; others are laypersons who minister in churches. This distinction is based on role and not on importance to the Lord's mission.

- Every believer is gifted by the Holy Spirit for ministry within the body of Christ and for service to lost persons outside the body.

- God calls every believer to some task somewhere in the world to work with Him to redeem people.

We have one Lord and one way of salvation. We have one message to preach and one call to repentance and faith.

Every believer is called of God to minister and is gifted by the Holy Spirit for ministry.

God Calls All Believers to Kingdom Advance Through Missions

When a church grows numerically, spiritually, and in ministry, believers become sensitive to the need to extend the gospel beyond their community to a world lost in sin. Their window on the world is enlarged, and they begin to see "fields white unto harvest." Their desire to witness, win, disciple, and minister is multiplied and enlarged.

God reaches down and calls out believers to go into the world with the message of redemption. For some believers, the call will be to their families, churches, and neighborhoods. Others will be called to go witness in faraway places. But all believers are commissioned to go into the world as their Lord's witnesses. Jesus declared:

"Just as the Father has sent Me, I also send you" (John 20:21).

How Shall the Lost Hear of Christ?

Believers in growing churches become burdened for the lost. They have an increased desire to carry the gospel to other places and to people of other cultures. This should not be surprising. It is a natural result of a church practicing kingdom principles. This is God's plan for establishing His kingdom.

The awesome fact is, those without Christ will never receive forgiveness and eternal life unless we share the gospel with them. Paul raised this startling reality with the church in Rome and with us:

"But how can they call on Him in whom they have not believed? And how can they believe without hearing about Him? And how can they hear without a preacher? And how can they preach unless they are sent? As it is written: 'How welcome are the feet of those who announce the gospel of good things!'" (Rom. 10:14-15).

Unless God calls us and we go, those who could be saved are hopelessly, eternally lost in sin and separation from God.

All believers are commissioned to go into the world as their Lord's witnesses.

Unless God calls us and we go, those who could be saved are hopelessly, eternally lost in sin and separation from God.

When Isaiah saw the Lord in His holy splendor, he confessed his sins and the sins of his people. He knew that the Lord God transcended anything he could ever know or experience. What Isaiah heard, however, was God calling out:

"Whom shall I send, and who will go for us?"

When Isaiah heard God's plea, the prophet responded:

"Here am I; send me" (Isa. 6:8).

This is God's call to all believers: "Whom shall I send?" Our response is to be: "Here am I; send me."

We will never know the Lord's heart until we see Him as a holy God who is sovereign over all things and who longs to reach out to persons who are separated from Him. Neither will we know God's heart until we recognize that He calls us to go in His name to share the good news with a lost world.

> We will never know the Lord's heart until we recognize that He calls us to go in His name to share the good news with a lost world.

God Grows Churches to Share the Gospel

God cares for each person in the world. He created each one and has a passion to save each one from eternal separation from Him. He raises up believers and grows churches to send them to those who have no hope and no message of salvation.

> A growing church cannot rest until it reaches the world for Christ.

A growing church cannot rest until it reaches the world for Christ, beginning in its own neighborhood and moving out nationally and internationally under the Holy Spirit's leadership and power.

Growing Churches Support Missions

A growing church will see the world as God sees it and will respond by sending its members into the world as missionaries. The church also will commit to pray and give so that the gospel can be spread across the world.

The Lord owns all He creates and provides all He owns to the redeemed. His resources for world missions

> A growing church will see the world as God sees it and will respond by sending its members into the world as missionaries.

are given through the lives of believers who become channels of support for missionaries at home and abroad.

A Growing Church Teaches Missions

Missions education is a significant ministry in growing churches. How will believers know to support missions if they are not taught? They must be discipled in kingdom advance just as much as they are in evangelism, discipleship, ministry, and fellowship.

A strong missions program must be supported by strong missions education. The lack of resources committed to missions in churches is due, in part, to the lack of missions education. This education should begin as early as possible with children, youth, and adults. God's people need to understand the nature of His kingdom and how it affects missions. They also need a fundamental understanding of the cost of discipleship, especially in areas of personal sacrifice and the responsibility for carrying the gospel to every person on the earth.

A growing church educates its members in kingdom advance as it provides opportunities for them to support missions through prayer and giving, and calls them out to serve the Lord as missionaries at home and across the globe. When a church becomes a "sending" church, gladly giving up sons and daughters, leaders and followers, and pastors and staff to missions, it is a growing church, contributing to kingdom advancement.

The *4* results of the *5* essential functions are:
Numerical Growth
Spiritual Transformation
Ministry Expansion
Kingdom Advance

The lack of resources committed to missions in churches is due, in part, to the lack of missions education.

When a church becomes a "sending" church, gladly giving up sons and daughters, leaders and followers, and pastors and staff to missions, it is a growing church.

5

CHURCH PRACTICE: PUTTING KINGDOM PRINCIPLES TOGETHER

The process of following kingdom principles to experience church growth is not new. It is as old as the Bible and as new as today's churches' needs. This book identifies and highlights this process as the *1·5·4 Principle*. Chapters 5 and 6 bond these eternal principles together to help believers and churches practice the biblical process of church growth.

Church practice grows out of the intentional strategy determined by the church and describes the balanced methodologies and essential actions a church employs to engage people in evangelism, discipleship, fellowship, ministry, and worship.

Is it possible to focus on the *1·5·4 Principle* in our churches and lives so that church growth occurs? Absolutely! You may ask, If I am not part of a growing church, what can I do to help my church grow? The following pages are devoted to this question.

ALWAYS PLACE DIVINE PROCESS AHEAD OF METHODS

Earlier, I cautioned that putting methods before the God-given process of church growth will endanger a church's long-term efforts to grow. You may have heard about a growth method another church successfully used. In an effort to help your church grow, you implemented that method in your church. You may or may not have succeeded. The *1·5·4 Principle* encourages you to begin with biblical *principles* and *process* rather than with methods. The *1·5·4 Principle* urges you to turn to the Scriptures and the essential principles of church growth to understand God's plan and to follow His directions in preparing for growth. The *1·5·4 Principle* will help you avoid trying to implement church growth methods that may fail you and lead to frustration and discouragement.

KINGDOM PRINCIPLES GUIDE OUR WORK

The hardest work in a church is work that does not work. It does not result in growing the body of Christ numerically, spiritually, in ministry, or in kingdom advancement. Haven't we all felt like we were going around in circles doing unproductive work?

Have you noticed how much church activity is cyclical? Each church year brings many of the same activities that we have done year after year. At the end of the year, we look back and discover that the activities have contributed little to the growth of the kingdom.

Someone said insanity is doing the same thing day after day, expecting different results. We laypersons and pastors do something like that year after year. We meet, plan, and work hard to grow our churches but experience little change.

When our frustration level gets high enough, we change methods. We seek to become innovative and creative. We frantically look for a method that has worked for someone else and implement it in our church immediately. We change the order and time of worship and Bible study, add services, begin new ministries, and change staff in an effort to make a fresh start and not to repeat our mistakes. Wouldn't it be better to stop being driven by our frustrations and give the kingdom principles of church growth a chance?

METHODS ARE NOT THE ANSWER TO OUR PROBLEMS

Methods are not the answer to ongoing church growth, because methods are not the problem. Methods are as different as the situations and people who use them. Methods are tools individuals and groups have developed in efforts to grow their churches. Nothing is wrong with or sacred about methods. Some work in one place and time; others work in many places over longer periods of time. Eventually, methods must change.

KINGDOM PRINCIPLES PRECEDE METHODS

Kingdom principles must be addressed first before meth-

Churches grow through the use of:

1 driving force:
The Great Commission

5 essential functions:
Evangelism
Discipleship
Fellowship
Ministry
Worship

4 results:
Numerical Growth
Spiritual Transformation
Ministry Expansion
Kingdom Advance

ods can be implemented successfully. Churches must be aware of how God works before they can work with Him.

GOD WORKS IN HIS OWN WAY

God is sovereign and often does not do things the way we think He should.

Have you heard someone say, "I've studied the great revivals and this is how God works"? A study of revivals is helpful and encouraging; but true revivals come when God intervenes in His divine, sovereign grace, not by employing certain methods.

God builds His kingdom through each church by working in His way and time for His purposes. We cannot and should not try to predict how the Lord will work to redeem people in our neighborhoods or in cultures across the world.

We should spend a great deal of time with God, individually and in our churches, praying and listening to Him. He is working throughout the world to redeem people to Himself, and we must learn to watch what He is doing around us in order to join Him.

We should look around to see how God is convicting people of their sins, how He is opening their lives to Christ, and how they are being prepared to receive Christ by faith. God uses all kinds of circumstances, especially failure and crisis, to melt the hearts of people who are separated from Him. They listen to the gospel and watch believers' lives. The Holy Spirit convicts them of their sins, and by God's grace, many respond in faith to Christ.

> We must learn what God is doing in our world in order to join Him.

GOD USES CHRISTIANS TO REACH THE LOST

God has chosen to use Christians and churches to reach the unsaved around the world. Our lives and churches must be aligned with His will if we are to be used by Him to redeem a world lost in sin.

If we harbor sin in our lives, the Lord cannot use us. When a church's fellowship is broken or when compromise is allowed to enter, the church's ministry is affected adversely. No method will overcome spiritual weakness and sin in our lives or in the lives of our churches. Only

> Our lives and churches must be aligned with God's will if we are to be used by Him to redeem a world lost in sin.

God's grace, forgiveness, restoration, and power can do that.

REPENTANCE: A KEY TO BEING USED OF GOD

The practice of repeating the cycle of sin, judgment, repentance, restoration, and blessing in our lives follows the pattern often found in Israel. After a time of experiencing the power and presence of God, Israel often fell away from Him, stopped keeping His commandments, stopped walking in His ways, and stopped worshiping Him. The Lord warned His people to repent and return to Him, often to no avail. After He punished them, they repented and returned to Him only to fall away again and repeat the cycle.

The prophets sounded this familiar message:

Repentance and rededication are the pathway to usefulness in God's kingdom (2 Chron. 7:14).

"To what purpose is the multitude of your sacrifices unto me? saith the Lord: I am full of the burnt offerings of rams, and the fat of fed beasts; and I delight not in the blood of bullocks, or of lambs, or of he goats" (Isa. 1:11).

"Come now, and let us reason together, saith the Lord: though your sins be as scarlet, they shall be as white as snow; though they be red like crimson, they shall be as wool" (Isa. 1:18).

"Therefore I will judge you, O house of Israel, every one according to his ways, saith the Lord God. Repent, and turn yourselves from all your transgressions; so iniquity shall not be your ruin" (Ezek. 18:30).

"Will the Lord be pleased with thousands of rams, or with ten thousands of rivers of oil? shall I give my firstborn for my transgression, the fruit of my body for the sin of my soul? He hath shown thee, O man, what is good; and what doth the Lord require of thee, but to do justly, and to love mercy, and to walk humbly with thy God?" (Mic. 6:7-8).

John spoke this same theme:

CHURCH PRACTICE: PUTTING KINGDOM PRINCIPLES TOGETHER

"Remember then how far you have fallen; repent, and do the works you did at first. Otherwise, I will come to you and remove your lampstand from its place — unless you repent" (Rev. 2:5).

KINGDOM PRINCIPLES REQUIRE OBEDIENCE

Kingdom principles demand that God's people, individually and congregationally, be what God wants them to be. When God demands that our lives be holy and surrendered to Him, He will not accept anything less. We are not required to be perfect; but we are required to be dedicated, obedient, and set apart to Him.

The Lord knew we could not be perfect. Therefore, He sent His Son to do His perfect will. Jesus provides everything we need to live in fellowship with God and one another. The Spirit lives in us to lead us to know and do God's will so that we may have fellowship with Him.

When we confess our sins, we receive instant forgiveness and are restored to a proper relationship with God. We have no excuse for living in disobedience to Him when He provides everything we need.

WE MUST WALK IN FELLOWSHIP WITH THE LORD

We have every resource we need to grow spiritually, evangelize the world, minister, and disciple believers. We have the power of God present through the Holy Spirit. We have Jesus Christ as our Advocate, Intercessor, and Lord. We have the Father's promise of guidance and success.

When we walk in fellowship with the Lord, He uses us to do great things. Being out of fellowship with Him keeps us from using His resources to fulfill the Great Commission. When our fellowship with our Lord is in disrepair, we miss His leadership and power in our lives and in the ministry of our churches.

Why many churches fail to grow is no mystery. Their failure can be traced to broken fellowship — with the Lord and one another. Church growth methods must accompany and be in harmony with our experience with God and our commitment to live and do as He says.

We are not required to be perfect, but we are required to be dedicated, obedient, and set apart to God.

Many churches' failure to grow can be traced to broken fellowship.

Church growth begins with practicing kingdom principles. You may ask how these principles can be practiced in your life and in your church. The following diagram and explanations of church practice will provide direction for practicing these growth principles.

THE PROCESS
OF CHURCH GROWTH

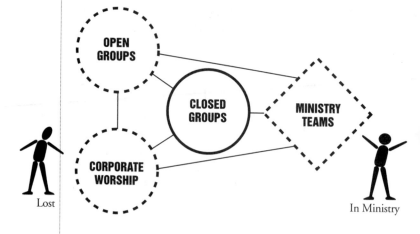

The drawing shows a person standing outside the four geometric figures. He represents a lost person the Lord wants to redeem. He may or may not have any religious interest, and his name could be on a church roll. We are to join the Lord in seeking this person's redemption.

This person, lost in sin and separated from God, may live next door to you, work with you, or live in another city, state, or country. He knows nothing of God's love, grace, forgiveness, or eternal life. He knows nothing of God's way of bringing people back to Himself.

CENTRAL FOCUS: THOSE WITHOUT CHRIST

This person is the center of our focus. If we show no concern for this person, we reject God's will. To turn our backs on this person by not providing him an opportunity to be saved is to fail to use kingdom principles.

Sometimes, with the Holy Spirit's help this person will come to us; but usually he will not. He may know something is wrong but may not know that he is lost or what to do about it.

In spite of people's religion, interest in God, or high morals, they never can achieve what only God can give. Someone must open the truth of the gospel to them, because they are dead to God and the things of God.

"As it is written: There is no one righteous, not even one; There is no one who understands, there is no one who seeks God. All have turned away, together they have become useless; there is no one who does good, there is not even one" (Rom. 3:10-12).

GOD PURSUES THE LOST

The Great Commission focuses on reaching lost people with the message of Christ so they can repent of their sins and be saved. Christ seeks the lost in a variety of ways; but in every instance, the gospel must be declared to them (Rom. 1:16; 10:14). Churches and believers must find ways to engage lost people, to witness to them, and to lead them to Christ.

CHURCH PRACTICE

Church practice grows out of the intentional strategy determined by the church and describes the balanced strategies and essential actions a church employs to engage people in evangelism, discipleship, fellowship, ministry, and worship.

Examining church practice requires a church to wrestle with the question, "What do we intend to be, where do we want to go, and what is the most effective way to do our work that makes the greatest difference in the lives of people?"

For many churches, strategy is not intentional and often nonexistent. Few leaders in the church may think about an intentional strategy. Most people are so busy doing church that they lose sight of the big picture. In the context of a local church, "strategy" describes the clear and deliberate intentions of the church, that when

> Someone must open the truth of the gospel to them, because they are dead to God and the things of God.

> Church practice grows out of the intentional strategy determined by the church.

woven together as a whole, drive the decisions about what purposeful work the church engages in and how to go about doing it. Strategy starts with the church's vision and values and identifies the church practice that is required for the church to achieve its objective in its distinctive environment. Vision is a compelling image of an achievable future. Strategy is the course the church decides to take; church practice is its operational plans to get there.

If the strategies and practices developed in a church are only human ideas and plans, a church can lose sight of its kingdom stewardship. A church can also lose the power, presence, and freshness of the Holy Spirit to direct the church according to God's will and in the ministries He chooses for the church. Nothing is wrong with a church being engaged in strategies and practices and ministries. However, they may or may not be the will of God for a particular church at a particular time unless the church has sought and found God's will in the endeavors in which it wishes to engage. The Holy Spirit is the church's guide, resource, and power to do the work the Father gives to the church.

> Church practices are dynamic and flexible and reflect individual church context, style, and cultural traditions.

The strategy and practice adopted by the church translates into forms or structures, work, leadership, participants, and the resources needed. It becomes the church's practical ministry action plan. Church practices are dynamic and flexible and reflect individual church context, style, and cultural traditions.

Take a closer look at Jesus' model of ministry outlined in Matthew 9:35-38 to consider how these strategies could be applied in the church. The example taught and demonstrated by Jesus Himself serves to instruct church leaders today on the need to build a biblically-balanced model of ministry in the church. According to this passage, Jesus initiated at least four basic strategies to accomplish His purpose.

"Then Jesus went to all the towns and villages, teaching in their synagogues, preaching the good news of the kingdom, and healing every disease and every sickness" (Matt. 9:35).

CHURCH PRACTICE: PUTTING KINGDOM PRINCIPLES TOGETHER

A corporate worship strategy exists for believers to *celebrate* God's grace and mercy, to *proclaim* God's truth, and to *evangelize* the lost in an atmosphere of encountering the presence, holiness, and revelation of Almighty God.

"When he saw the crowds, He felt compassion for them, because they were weary and worn out, like sheep without a shepherd" (Matt. 9:36).

An open group strategy exists to lead people to faith in the Lord Jesus Christ and to build on mission Christians by engaging people in *foundational* evangelism, discipleship, ministry, fellowship, and worship through ongoing, *evangelistic Bible study* units of believers together with unbelievers in an atmosphere of compassion to share the gospel.

"Then He said to His disciples, 'The harvest is abundant, but the workers are few'" (Matt. 9:37).

A closed group strategy exists to *build kingdom leaders* and to *equip believers to serve* by engaging people in discipleship that moves them toward spiritual transformation through short-term, self-contained training units in an atmosphere of *accountability* to God and to each other.

"Therefore, pray to the Lord of the harvest to send out workers into His harvest" (Matt. 9:38).

A ministry team strategy exists to build up the body of Christ to accomplish the work of *service* within the church and to be involved in *missions* outside the church through new or existing *kingdom units* in an atmosphere of prayer and urgency for people in need of God's love.

Jesus initiated at least four basic strategies for a balanced church minstry:
- Open Groups
- Corporate Worship
- Closed Groups
- Ministry Teams

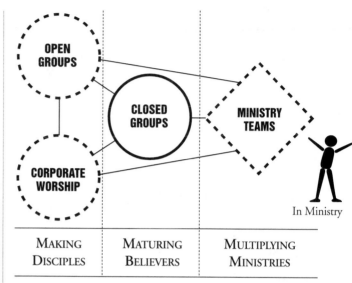

Lost

In Ministry

MAKING DISCIPLES	MATURING BELIEVERS	MULTIPLYING MINISTRIES

Effective church practice involves three stages — making disciples, maturing believers, and multiplying ministries.

Effective church practice involves three stages — Making Disciples, Maturing Believers, and Multiplying Ministries — and employs at least these four basic strategies to carry out the work of the church:

1. Open Groups
2. Corporate Worship
3. Closed Groups
4. Ministry Teams

MAKING DISCIPLES: **Open Groups** and **Corporate Worship** are the foundational strategies that serve as entry points into the church for unbelievers. These strategies represent making disciples and assimilating them into one body of Christ. The dotted circles on the visual diagram depict that these strategies are entry points.

MATURING BELIEVERS: **Closed Groups** represent the maturing stage that continues and intensifies the assimilation process for new believers and members. The circle on the visual diagram is solid to depict this closed concept.

MULTIPLYING MINISTRIES: **Ministry Teams** represent the multiplying stage that provides members with opportunities for service and missions and to start kingdom units. This stage also serves as an entry point into the church for unbelievers as believers minister to their needs. The diamond on the visual diagram also is dotted to depict an entry point. The left angle of the diamond points inward for service in the church, and the right angle points outward for missions outside the church.

The three stages of church practice — Making Disciples, Maturing Believers, and Multiplying Ministries — also can be viewed as the three broad stages in the process of spiritual transformation that need to take place in a disciple's life.

Becoming a Disciple:
- Participating in Bible study as the foundational step of discipleship
- Experiencing fellowship with other believers
- Beginning assimilation into the church

Maturing As a Believer:
- Learning to be a leader
- Receiving training and equipping for ministry
- Developing accountability and continuing assimilation

Multiplying Ministries:
- Participating in ministry through service in the church
- Participating in ministry through missions outside the church
- Multiplying themselves in and through others

To guide Christians through the three stages of discipleship, churches could provide ministry development in this pattern:

1. New Christians learn the basics of following Christ and being involved in ministry.
2. Believers observe other believers in ministry.
3. Believers first minister under guidance and supervision of a mature believer.
4. Believers minister independently and multiply themselves in and through others.

A church model is unlike any secular model. A church, the people of God, is built upon a covenant relationship with God. A covenant relationship suggests a faithful promise or binding pledge under seal. Forgiveness by God is central to the covenant. The covenant response by the people comes from a transformed heart. "I will put my law in their minds and write it on their hearts. I will be their God, and they will be my people," declared Jeremiah of God's new covenant (Jer. 31:33, NIV). Jesus fulfilled God's promise, creating a people for Himself. God's expectations from His people of righteousness, holiness, worship, and service are woven into this covenant relationship.

The writer of Hebrews pointed to Christ as the mediator of the new covenant.

> *"How much more will the blood of the Messiah, who through the eternal Spirit offered Himself without blemish to God, cleanse our consciences from dead works to serve the living God? Therefore He is the mediator of a new covenant, so that those who are called might receive the promise of the eternal inheritance, because a death has taken place for redemption from the transgressions committed under the first covenant" (Heb. 9:14-15).*

Paul taught the church at Corinth about their core role in that:

> *"He has made us competent as ministers of a new covenant" (2 Cor. 3:6).*

> A church model is unlike any secular model. A church, the people of God, is built upon a covenant relationship with God.

6

CHURCH PRACTICE: MAKING, MATURING, AND MULTIPLYING

I n Chapter 5, we provided an overview of the process of church growth. We saw how applying God's principles of growth to church practice could accomplish our goal of reaching the lost person outside the four geometric figures. In this chapter, we will expand our discussion, further defining these three stages of growth — making, maturing, and multiplying.

Our central focus remains on the person without Christ. Our guide is the intentional strategy determined by the church. The model for church practice provides physical evidence of our focus, strategy, and the underlying Kingdom principles of growth.

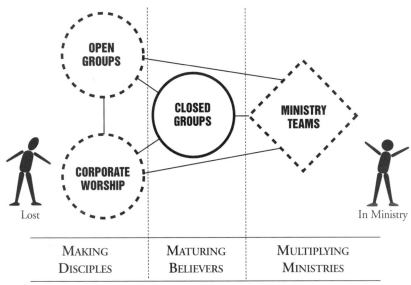

The open group is a foundational strategy that serves as an entry point into the church for unbelievers.

An open group should be defined by its purpose, nature, function, and participants rather than by its resources, label, time frame, or location.

OPEN-GROUP BIBLE STUDY: AN ESSENTIAL STRATEGY

An open-group strategy exists to lead people to faith in the Lord Jesus Christ and to build on-mission Christians by engaging people in foundational evangelism, discipleship, ministry, fellowship, and worship through ongoing, evangelistic Bible study units of believers together with unbelievers in an atmosphere of compassion to share the gospel.

The open group is a foundational strategy that serves as an entry point into the church for unbelievers. This strategy represents the "beginning" stage of the assimilation process for new believers and members. The dotted circle on the visual diagram (page 101) depicts this strategy as an entry point.

An open group is primarily an evangelistic Bible study group or event comprised of an intentional mix of both believers and unbelievers. The focus is evangelism, the context is Bible study, and the intent is to begin assimilation. It is also a great environment for building relationships and encouragement. Participants can enter the group at any point. Requisite knowledge of the content being studied by the group is not required.

An open group also emphasizes the sending out of people on mission outside the church and multiplying leaders of new groups for service in the church.

An open group should be defined by its purpose, nature, function, and participants rather than by its resources, label, time frame, or location. "Open" means both believers and unbelievers are invited to participate in a Bible study class, department, study group, small group, cell group, or event that has an intentional evangelistic purpose —every time the group meets. An open group is an eternal touch point where the lost of the world come together with the saved of the world so that the Savior of the world can advance His kingdom by bringing people to salvation. Open groups are conduits of the gospel enterprise, receiving, assimilating, multiplying, providing a base of discipling, and then sending out.

An evangelistic Bible study group is a group intentionally formed around the study of God's Word. This is different from a group that gathers for support, fellowship, leadership training, or skill development that often requires requisite knowledge of the content being studied. Bible study groups that are designed primarily for reaching lost people are open groups. Bible study groups that are designed primarily for moving saved people toward spiritual maturity and transformation are closed groups.

Sunday School, as an expression of the open-group concept, is recommended as the best proven organizational framework for involving families and individuals in the evangelistic work of the church. The Sunday School is time-tested, having endured massive cultural and societal pressures placed on it from the world.

Transferable Principles for Open Groups

The concept of the open group helps the church do the work of the Great Commission — mobilizing, assimilating, and teaching believers so that they become disciples of Christ.

If an open group is to fulfill its objective, church leaders must champion and communicate the objective in a clear, compelling manner. The following five transferable principles undergird the open group concept and represent priorities to be addressed. They will be valuable as primary messages that guide the effectiveness of an open group. Because these principles are transferable and cross-cultural, they can and should be applied effectively regardless of the form or structure a church selects and in both church planting and in existing church situations.

The Principle of Foundational Evangelism — An ongoing, open group is the foundational evangelism strategy of the church.

Ongoing, open Bible study groups that reproduce new groups provide the best long-term approach for building a ministry environment that guides preschoolers and children toward conversion through foundational teaching, encourages unsaved people to come to faith in Christ, assimilates new believers into the life of the church, and encourages believers to lead others to Christ.

> Sunday School is recommended as the best proven organizational framework for involving families and individuals in the evangelistic work of the church.

Open groups provide the most efficient churchwide evangelism training network to equip members to become passionate soul-winners.

Open groups implemented through short-term groups and through special Bible teaching events are effective ways to promote outreach and evangelism and to address specific life concerns, spiritual issues, church functions, and doctrinal issues. These groups create a great center for missionary power as people tell and live the wondrous story of Christ's redeeming love.

The Principle of Foundational Discipleship — Knowing God through Jesus is the first step of discipleship. An open group is a seven-day-a-week process, and Bible study is a foundational step of discipleship for involving people in seeking the kingdom of God and fulfilling the Great Commission.

Open groups provide the primary organizational framework for involving families and individuals in the comprehensive work of the church including evangelism, discipleship, fellowship, ministry, and worship.

These groups provide foundational discipleship and encourage members to strengthen their Christian walk by participating in other discipleship opportunities.

Open groups emphasize that every member who is a believer must become accountable for the responsibility God has given him or her as a minister and missionary to the world. Open groups support all church ministries and intentionally encourage its participants to be good stewards, fully involved in the church's overall mission.

The Principle of Family Responsibility —The open group affirms the home as the center of biblical guidance.

Open groups help equip Christian parents, including single parents, to fulfill their responsibility as the primary Bible teachers and disciplers of their children. They encourage Christian parents who by word and deed guide their children to integrate the Scriptures into their lives influencing how they think and act.

Open groups involve families in the comprehensive work of the church. They work to nurture sound, healthy families and seek to lead non-Christian parents to Christ.

Open groups provide the most efficient churchwide evangelism training network to equip members to become passionate soul-winners.

Bible study is a foundational step of discipleship for involving people in seeking the kingdom of God and fulfilling the Great Commission.

Open groups help equip Christian parents, including single parents, to fulfill their responsibility as the primary Bible teachers and disciplers of their children.

CHURCH PRACTICE: MAKING, MATURING, & MULTIPLYING

The Principle of Spiritual Transformation — The open group engages learners in the biblical model of instruction that begins to lead people toward spiritual transformation.

Open groups affirm that spiritual transformation is God's work of changing a believer into the likeness of Jesus by creating a new identity in Christ and by empowering a lifelong relationship of love, trust, and obedience to glorify God.

Open groups champion the absolute truth and authority of the Word of God and compel believers to integrate a biblical worldview into their minds, hearts, and lives through ongoing systematic Bible study.

Open groups recognize that Bible study is most effective when it occurs in the context of the learner's total life, especially family relationships, and when it considers the special needs, generational perspective, age and life-stage characteristics, and learning styles of the learner. These groups address transcultural life issues common to individuals, churches, families, tribes, and nations regardless of geographic, ethnic, or language identity.

> Spiritual transformation is God's work of changing a believer into the likeness of Jesus.

The Principle of Biblical Leadership — The open group calls for leaders to follow the biblical standard of leadership.

Open groups affirm the pastor as the primary leader in its ministry of building on-mission Christians. Open groups call leaders to a prophetic ministry, listening to God's voice, discovering His message, integrating the message into their lives, and proclaiming His truth through His church to the nations.

Open groups recognize that the leader is the lesson in that every leader is accountable for being an authentic example of Christianity in personal living and producing new leaders for service through the ministries of the church. Open groups recognize that planning is essential in implementing its strategy.

Basic Structures for Open Groups

At least two specific kinds of open evangelistic Bible study groups could be implemented by a church: ongoing Bible study groups and short-term Bible study groups.

As a church establishes its goals and defines its purpose, it may choose to use a combination of both groups. Ongoing Bible study groups could be compared to the interstate highway system; they are best for helping a church achieve its long-range goals. They provide the foundational infrastructure of the church's ministry. Short-term Bible study groups could be thought of as the local highway system; they provide the church with flexibility and facilitate access to the church's "interstate" of ongoing Bible study.

Ongoing Open Bible Study Groups — Ongoing Bible study groups have no specified end date and focus on reaching the unsaved, building relationships, and promoting spiritual growth, with the goal of starting new Bible study groups and developing leaders for those groups.

Short-term Open Bible Study Groups or Events — Short-term Bible study groups are started with a specified end date and focus on reaching the unsaved, building relationships, and promoting spiritual growth, with the goal of transitioning participants into an ongoing Bible study group. These groups often meet where a more informal and intimate environment can be created and often appeal to unreached people who will not attend a group "at the church." Examples could include Vacation Bible School; mission VBS; evangelistic Bible study during the weekday in a business setting, in apartment complexes, in retirement villages, in nursing homes, in prison facilities; and equal access Bible clubs in public schools.

As much as an open group has to offer, it is only the starting line on the journey of faith.

As much as an open group has to offer, it is only the starting line on the journey of faith. It only addresses the beginning point in the process of spiritual transformation. As an agent of spiritual transformation, the church must encourage people to continue in their journey in the closed group experience. Viewing open groups and closed groups as collaborative strategies will ensure a more balanced church practice.

Corporate Worship: an Essential Strategy

Worship that transforms is the response of believers to the presence, holiness, and revelation of Almighty God. We need to recognize that worship is an essential part of a church's evangelistic and discipling ministry. Worship services must be designed for believers and for people we seek to reach for Christ.

Worship and small-group Bible study have proven effective for centuries in reaching lost persons. Worship and Bible study are two places where believers and non-believers can easily mingle. Churches should have a strategy of worship and Bible study that includes members and unbelievers. Worship is a foundational strategy that serves as an entry point into the church for unbelievers. This strategy represents the making disciples stage of the assimilation process for new believers and members.

Intent of worship. — The form of worship is not as important as the purpose of worship. We encounter God in worship and are changed by His presence.

Cultures and people are different. Worship styles also differ. Some people worship quietly; others shout praises to the Lord. Some churches use hymnbooks; others sing from memory or use chorus sheets. Some people lift up their hands in worship; others kneel with heads bowed and eyes closed. How we worship are expressions of how we feel and how we express those feelings to God. *That* we worship is far more important than *how* we worship.

Meeting people's spiritual and emotional needs should be the people-centered intent of every worship service. God is the object and subject of worship, but people are to be ministered to in worship services.

Review the eight Elements of Worship presented on pages 59-65.

Importance of worship. — The importance of worship cannot be overemphasized. The gospel must be declared in worship to evangelize the lost. Believers need to hear

CORPORATE WORSHIP

We need to recognize that worship is an essential part of a church's evangelistic and discipling ministry.

the gospel to strengthen their faith and to motivate them to share Christ's love with all people.

Worship involves ministry. — Worship is ministry to the Lord and to those who attend worship services. Worship is described in the Bible as service to the Lord. Paul called the sacrifice of our bodies and lives to the Lord our "spiritual worship."

"Therefore, brothers, by the mercies of God, I urge you to present your bodies as a living sacrifice, holy and pleasing to God; this is your spiritual worship. Do not be conformed to this age, but be transformed by the renewing of your mind, so that you may discern what is the good, pleasing, and perfect will of God" (Rom. 12:1-2).

Worship is united by fellowship. — Fellowship unites believers with the Lord and with one another. Fellowship is the expression of love between believers and between believers and God. It is a testimony of God's power to save and to break down barriers between people. Fellowship is never richer than when the body of Christ gathers and believers can see brothers and sisters in Christ singing, praying, praising God, and listening to His Word.

The physical closeness of people gathered in a worship service adds to their sense of comfort, joy, and assurance. Separated from each other through the week, believers gather in unity and love to worship God and to fellowship with one another.

A worship service must be designed to meet the fellowship needs of the church. Regardless of how worshipers in your church greet one another — with a handshake, words of greeting, or a hug — time must be given for every person to reach out to others in love. Fellowship creates a family spirit in the family of God. Without this spirit, the "family" will be only a group gathered.

Worship that transforms calls individuals present to respond. Whether this response is shared with others present or is a private response of the heart, it leads to a lifestyle change. When unbelievers are present, God seeks to draw them to Himself as they observe believers participating in worship.

> Fellowship is a testimony of God's power to save and to break down barriers between people.

Leadership Implications

The leadership responsible for congregational worship must understand and communicate that God has designed the elements of worship as a means for God's people to know Him and thus experience spiritual transformation.

As the largest "meeting" of the church, congregational worship has unique impact on the body life of the church. Through this joint meeting, God transforms His people.

Congregational worship is an essential event in the life of a church and should be given priority time, energy, and prayer. The leader has the primary responsibility for helping the congregation to focus on God, which creates the unity necessary for church health and growth. Worship includes leading people to celebrate the advancement of the Kingdom of God and to commit themselves to go into the world to carry out the Great Commission.

As the leader of the church, the pastor is the primary worship leader. He must take the responsibility to provide an environment that facilitates spiritual transformation in the lives of believers. He must involve others in planning and leading worship. Worship must be led by worship leaders who are themselves being spiritually transformed, understand their role, and have a growing kingdom focus.

Worship must be planned, and the planning process includes an understanding of the congregation. Worship that transforms is planned with a focus on God. Planning begins with asking "why?" regarding every element of the worship experience. Planning includes an intentional effort to balance and integrate the elements of worship. Whatever forms or methods are used in biblical worship, God will be honored and people will be transformed.

Opportunities for prompting during worship should be seen as teaching moments, not just announcements. ("Now we will give our tithes and offerings to God as a response of obedient stewardship, gratitude, and trust." rather than "Now, we will receive the offering.")

Leadership must understand and communicate that God has designed the elements of worship as a means for God's people to know Him and thus experience spiritual transformation.

As the leader of the church, the pastor is the primary worship leader.

Worship must be planned with an intentional effort to balance and integrate the elements of worship.

CLOSED GROUPS

Closed groups represent the maturing stage that continues and intensifies the assimilation process for new believers and members.

CLOSED GROUPS: AN ESSENTIAL STRATEGY

A closed-group strategy exists to build kingdom leaders and to equip believers to serve by engaging people in discipleship that moves them toward spiritual transformation through short-term, self-contained training units in an atmosphere of accountability to God and to each other.

Closed groups represent the maturing stage that continues and intensifies the assimilation process for new believers and members. The circle on the visual diagram (page 101) is solid to depict this closed concept.

A closed group primarily is an equipping group or event comprised of believers only; the focus is training, the context is discipling, and the intent is to continue assimilation.

A closed group is composed of believers that covenant together to meet over a short period of time for the purpose of becoming equipped to accomplish the objectives of the church.

The greatest threat to the church today is the loss of discipleship-building ministries where mature, spiritually transformed Christians are multiplying themselves through other people. The loss of discipleship-building ministries in our churches can be underscored this way: "If you were to lead your neighbor to Christ today, in three years would you want that person to be like the average Christian?" The Great Commission emphasizes both evangelism and discipleship. Evangelism is foremost; discipleship feeds evangelism.

If evangelism — the process of sharing the gospel with lost persons and winning people to Christ enabling them to enter the kingdom of God — is the focus of an open group, then what is discipleship and how is a church involved in discipling through closed groups?

Discipleship is a lifelong journey of obedience to Christ that transforms a person's values and behavior and results in ministry in one's home, church, and world.

Discipling is the process of teaching the new citizen in the kingdom of God to love, trust, and obey God the King and how to win and train others to do the same.

Discipleship is a lifelong journey of obedience to Christ that transforms a person's values and behavior and results in ministry.

Closed groups function within the framework of the comprehensive church strategy. Jesus surrounded Himself with a closed group of twelve men. He was their Teacher; they were His disciples. The twelve apostles remained a closed group for three years before they dispersed to multiply followers of The Way. The group was closed, but the cause — the larger movement — was open to others.

Closed groups have a specific purpose. During the three years Jesus traveled with, ministered in the presence of, and taught within their hearing, the apostles lived each day with a purpose. They were being equipped to become followers of Christ, to become leaders in His church, and to minister in His name. And the apostles covenanted together to follow Jesus to learn what that meant and how that would be accomplished.

Closed groups are closed for a period of time. Requisite knowledge of the content being studied by the group often is required — participants cannot enter the group at any point. The disciples were together during the three years of Jesus' life on earth. When Jesus returned to be with His Heavenly Father, the disciples dispersed to carry out the kingdom agenda. The group did not remain closed but instead multiplied many times over as they scattered to carry the Gospel to others. Christ's mission was accomplished because the disciples did not remain a closed group.

Transferable Principles for Closed Groups

The Relationship Principle — Transformation takes place in relationships. All relationships start with and are based on an intimate relationship with Jesus. Also, transformational discipleship expresses itself in other relationships including marriage, family, friendships, church, work, acquaintances, community, and society. A church looks for ways to develop and encourage such relationships. "He said to him, 'You shall love the Lord your God with all your heart, with all your soul, and with all your mind.' This is the greatest and most important commandment. The second is like it: 'You shall love your neighbor as yourself.' All the Law and the Prophets depend on these two commandments" (Matt. 22:37-40).

The Followship Principle — Jesus calls every believer to follow Him. The church provides a spiritually sensitive environment that encourages believers to respond to Jesus' call to follow, challenges them to fulfill that call in the Body of Christ, and develops their skills for service. Jesus glorified the Father by fulfilling His call. "I have glorified You on the earth by completing the work You gave Me to do" (John 17:4).

The Empowerment Principle — Believers must be empowered to serve. Throughout His ministry Jesus empowered, equipped, discipled, trained, built up, developed, and prepared His disciples to serve. The Holy Spirit empowers the church to develop servant leaders who depend on His power. Believers use their spiritual gift(s) to equip others. For example, those who don't have the gift of mercy are still called to be merciful. The one best equipped to teach and train them about mercy is the one with that gift! "And He personally gave some to be apostles, some prophets, some evangelists, some pastors and teachers, for the training of the saints in the work of ministry, to build up the body of Christ, until we all reach unity in the faith and in the knowledge of God's Son, growing into a mature man with a stature measured by Christ's fullness. Then we will no longer be little children, tossed by the waves and blown around by every wind of teaching, by human cunning with cleverness in the techniques of deceit. But speaking the truth in love, let us grow in every way into Him who is the Head — Christ. From Him the whole body, fitted and knit together by every supporting ligament, promotes the growth of the body for building up itself in love by the proper working of each individual part" (Eph. 4:11-16).

The Flexibility Principle — Diverse people need flexible and adaptable ways to experience spiritual transformation. Spiritual transformation is unique to each individual who has a personal relationship with Jesus. A church ensures that its organizations, structures, processes,

Spiritual transformation is unique to each individual who has a personal relationship with Jesus.

procedures, and systems facilitate the Holy Spirit's work of spiritual transformation. This includes methods and messages appropriate for people of all learning styles, personality types, genders, ages, family types and situations, cultural differences, economic conditions, and ethnic backgrounds. The Gospels record various approaches Jesus used to disciple diverse people.

The Lifestyle Principle — Transformed believers naturally express biblical examples and insights in everyday life. Jesus left us the supreme example that we should follow in His steps (1 Peter 2:21). The bulk of Scripture is the story of diverse, ordinary, common people who demonstrated a life transformed by God. Transformed disciples comfortably express what God is doing in their lives, their families, and the world. God uses biblical, historical, and contemporary examples to teach us to experience Him.

Thus, churches encourage believers to share their spiritual stories with family, friends, and others in natural ways. Each believer, regardless of age or length of time as a Christian, is a unique treasure from God with a story to share. "These commandments that I give you today are to be upon your hearts. Impress them on your children. Talk about them when you sit at home and when you walk along the road, when you lie down and when you get up" (Deut. 6:6-7, NIV).

The Accountability Principle — Every believer is accountable to God. A church teaches believers to obey everything Jesus commanded (Matt. 28:20). "So then, each of us will give an account of himself to God" (Rom. 14:12). The measure of discipleship is the degree to which a believer is like Jesus in attitudes, behavior, and relationships. Although believers are accountable to God, God uses spouses, other family members, church members, friends, and others to keep each of us aware of our accountability to Him.

"You shall love the Lord your God with all your heart, with all your soul, with all your strength, and with all your mind; and your neighbor as yourself" (Luke 10:27).

> Transformed disciples comfortably express what God is doing in their lives, their families, and the world.

Basic Structures for Closed Groups

The best structures for closed groups that focus on equipping need to be determined by the local church. Structures for closed groups in a church primarily include several short-term tracks and events for training church members including:

Leadership Training Track — Groups intentionally organized to train the lay leadership in the church for volunteer leadership positions in open groups, closed groups, corporate worship, committees, and so forth. These could be ongoing or regular meetings such as the weekly meeting for open group leaders.

Evangelism Training Track — Groups intentionally organized to train open group leaders and participants in evangelism and to engage the participants in ongoing evangelistic experiences.

Ministry Equipping Track — Groups intentionally organized for a short-term period for the purpose of training people for a specific ministry experience or assignment. Examples include training youth to conduct a mission Vacation Bible School, training parents to serve as counselors on a mission trip, and training adults who have volunteered for a medical missions assignment. See the Ministry Teams section on pages 116 ff. for other examples of the types of ministry training.

Age-Group Ministries Track — Groups intentionally organized for age-group learners including preschoolers, children, youth, collegiates, young adults, singles, seniors, and other adults.

Music Development Track — Groups intentionally organized for age-group learners for training in music development including preschoolers, children, youth, young adults, and adult choirs and related instrumental groups.

Women's Enrichment Track — Groups intentionally organized for women to equip women to enrich the lives of other women and their families for Christ, to enable women to discover their God-given gifts for ministry, to search out the needs in their churches and communities and match those needs with their own gifts of service, to lead women to accept Christ as Lord, to become women

Structures for closed groups in a church primarily include several short-term tracks and events for training church members.

114

of deeper prayer, and to become women who study the Bible and base their entire lives on the Word of God.

Men's Ministry Track — Groups intentionally organized for men to discover how they are uniquely called and shaped by God to live the Great Commandment and to equip men to fulfill the Great Commission in every aspect of their lives — personal, home, church, workplace, community, and the world.

Missions Education Track — Groups intentionally organized for age-group learners for training in missions education and missions experiences including preschoolers, children, youth, young adults, and adult.

Special Interests Track — Groups intentionally organized on the basis of learners' interests such as marriage enrichment, parenting skills, family issues, or prayer.

Special Needs Track — Groups intentionally organized on the basis of specific affinity and personal needs such as divorce recovery and health.

The Process of Spiritual Transformation in Closed Groups

The process of spiritual transformation continues to be shaped beyond the foundational open-group experience by building disciples through closed-group experiences. Spiritual transformation is a progressive change of worldview, values, attitudes, and behavior that brings glory to God. Spiritual transformation begins with a change of the heart by God in Christ and reaches out to touch the life and witness of God's people at every level of life.

Seven essential areas should be explored in a closed-group experience:
- The Kingdom of God
- Identity in Christ
- Relationships
- The Church
- The Work Place
- Spiritual Warfare
- The World

Through closed groups, believers explore critical biblical issues that affect their maturity in Christ. These areas can be explored in more depth in a closed group than in an open group. They are essential areas to develop in a believer's life that are necessary for a believer to become a multiplier.

The following are seven essential areas that should be explored in a closed-group experience: the kingdom of God, identity in Christ, relationships, the church, the work place, spiritual warfare, and the world.

MINISTRY TEAMS

Ministry teams represent the "multiplying" stage that provides members with opportunities for service and missions and to start kingdom units.

Individual Christians are best prepared for ministry as they participate in an open group, in worship experiences, and in a closed group. Equipped Christians join together in ministry to accomplish the mission of the church.

MINISTRY TEAMS: AN ESSENTIAL STRAGEGY

A ministry team strategy exists to build up the body of Christ to accomplish the work of service within the church and to be involved in missions outside the church through new or existing kingdom units in an atmosphere of prayer and urgency for people in need of God's love.

Ministry teams represent the multiplying stage that provides members with opportunities for service and missions and to start kingdom units. This stage also serves as an entry point into the church for unbelievers as believers minister to their needs. The diamond on the visual diagram (page 101) is dotted to depict an entry point. The left angle of the diamond points inward for service in the church, and the right angle points outward for missions outside the church.

The process of spiritual transformation that finds expression in open groups, corporate worship, and closed groups continues as people experience service and missions.

An understanding of Ephesians 4 suggests that individual Christians are best prepared for ministry as they participate in an open group, in worship experiences, and in a closed group. Then, within the context of the ministry of the local church, these equipped Christians join together to accomplish the mission of the church.

In the 1990s, there was a dramatic rise in the use of short-term, small-group studies designed to equip Christians for ministry. This increase in use suggests that there should be a corresponding strong increase in the work of individual Christians in the ministry of the churches.

Except for isolated instances, such as the rise in volunteers for short-term missions, there is no such increase. In fact, recent research projects show that far too many churches identify the need for workers in their existing ministries as being one of the greatest challenges that they face. These churches are seeking to expand their ministries through the efforts of a small number of willing workers.

This disconnect between the rise of closed-group studies, which should be equipping Christians for ministry, and the actual involvement of Christians in ministry begs for improvement in this area of church life. It underscores the need for a model of doing church that leads all Christians to the practice of doing ministry in the life of the church.

The church model and process discussed in this chapter, when implemented holistically, provides a framework for ministry teams that involves all Christians in the ministry of the church.

Many churches are known for having an emphasis on ministry to the church family. They are quick to minister to physical, emotional, and social needs of those who are a part of the congregation and its extended family. Other churches emphasize the need to minister beyond the walls of the church. They are known for evangelistic and/or social programs that focus on reaching people outside the congregation. Instead of having one of these two types of ministry efforts, it is important for churches to have a variety of ministry teams that accomplish these dual purposes.

Transferable Principles for Ministry Teams

The concept of ministry teams is applicable and transferable to virtually every church model in use today. It is a concept that can be seen throughout Scripture. From the moment when Jesus sent the twelve on the first assignments, to the choosing of the seven, to the ministry of Paul and Silas, the Bible teaches that Christians can and should join together to accomplish internal and external ministry.

In reality, every church model is actually using groups to accomplish much of their ministry. The critical difference is that there may not be an intentional strategy for the model selected and used.

The following principles can guide the implementation of an *intentional* ministry team strategy and can be applied to various church models:

The Principle of Filtering — Individual Christians are capable of conceiving untold numbers of possible ministry activities for the work of a church. If left unchecked, such ministry possibilities can keep the

> The Bible teaches that Christians can and should join together to accomplish internal and external ministry.

The church must filter out any ministry action which is not compatible with its purpose.

church very busy but accomplishing very little toward its biblical purpose. To keep the church and its ministries focused on work that is its calling, the church must filter out any ministry action which is not compatible with its purpose. When a ministry action meets three filtering criteria, it is appropriate for a church to develop a team to accomplish that ministry.

• Church ministry actions must be built on fulfilling the Great Commission (Matthew 28:19-20).

• Church ministry actions must be built on accomplishing one or more of the following biblical functions:
Evangelism (2 Corinthians 5:17-21)
Discipleship (Ephesians 2:8-10)
Fellowship (Acts 2:42, 46-47)
Ministry (Ephesians 4:11-15)
Worship (John 4:21-24)

• Church ministry actions must be built on achieving one or more of the following kingdom results:
Numerical Growth (Acts 2:41, 47)
Spiritual Transformation (2 Corinthians 3:18; John 13:31-17:26)
Ministry Expansion (Acts 6:1-3; 13:1-3)
Kingdom Advance (Acts 1:8; Matthew 6:33)

The Principle of Internal/External Focus — Church ministry teams can be focused on strengthening the church body or on sharing the love of Christ in the world. However, churches must have ministry teams that focus both internally and externally.

The Principle of Universal Involvement — Every Christian has a place of responsibility within the total ministry of the church. The concept of every Christian performing active ministry is found within the doctrine of the individual priesthood of the believer. Each Christian must accept responsibility for personal involvement in a ministry team.

The Principle of Ministry-Team Integration — All church open-group, corporate-worship, and closed-group activities are led by ministry teams. Churches integrate ministry teams within the life of the church as they staff the various ministries of the church. This principle leads persons to understand that their work is ministry, not just participation in an organization in the church. For example, church music is not a program. Instead, it is a ministry that leads the congregation to worship God more fully.

The Principle of Commission — Ministry teams are not an entity unto themselves. Ministry teams function under the commission or authorization of the church. The leadership of each ministry team is responsible for reporting the results/fruit of the team's ministry to the church.

Basic Structure of a Ministry Team

The dual purpose (internal and external focus) of ministry teams is expressed by the structures in which they exist. There is no specific, set structure for a ministry team. However, each ministry team has leadership and is accountable to the church. Structures for ministry teams are as varied as the church and community needs that they are designed to serve and must be determined by the individual church in light of its specific, cultural context and the balance of its other practices.

Throughout the book of Acts, Christians joined together under the umbrella of the church as they joined together to do the ministry to which God had called them. Paul's writings in Ephesians both describe and explain this joining together:

> 1 Corinthians 1:17 – Paul preached the gospel, but others baptized.
> 1 Corinthians 3:7-9 – We are fellow workers. Some plant; others water.

Following are some examples of some ministry teams, but the list is not exhaustive:
- Corporate worship planners
- Visitation ministries to nursing homes and prisons
- Sunday School classes and departments
- Evangelism trainers and participants
- Women's enrichment ministry

This principle leads persons to understand that their work is ministry, not just participation in an organization in the church.

Each ministry team has leadership and is accountable to the church.

- Prayer groups
- Children's ministry
- Collegiate ministry
- Senior adult ministry
- Special education
- Deacons
- Missions groups
- Adult choirs
- Church orchestra
- Handbell choirs
- Vacation Bible School
- Recreation/sports teams
- January Bible Study
- Television/Radio ministry
- Church library staff
- Parking attendants
- Meals to the homebound
- Church-wide fellowship/event planners
- Youth apprentices for various ministries
- Preschool ministry
- Youth Ministry
- Singles' ministry
- Men's ministry
- Family ministries
- Trustees
- Health ministries
- Age-graded choir leaders
- Praise bands
- Parenting groups
- Committees
- Health groups
- Publicity/outreach team
- Drama groups
- Ushers
- Greeters
- Benevolence groups

PROCESS AND ESSENTIAL ACTIONS

Biblically sound church practice — guided by equipped leaders who employ an intentional and integrated strategy of open groups, corporate worship, closed groups, and ministry teams — will achieve significant kingdom results in time. From a practical point of view, effective church practice is implemented through an ongoing process involving ten essential actions that guides the development of church practice. These actions are suggested to take place in the context of a comprehensive church-wide process rather than independent actions of the leadership. This approach underscores the value of a holistic plan, the interrelationship of the four church practice strategies, and the collaborative spirit desired by all the leaders.

These ten actions are given below as brief, concrete, imperative statements with descriptions enlarging the meaning of each best practice. Generally, the actions are listed in the sequence in which they would be implemented, but the sequence should not be overemphasized.

Effective church practice is implemented through an ongoing process involving ten essential actions.

1. Commit to the Strategy

We will commit to a holistic and comprehensive strategy of the church by:

- Renewing our commitment to the Great Commission.
- Developing a church model that stands on biblical principles, reflects the church's unique context, applies effective church practices, and achieves kingdom results.
- Engaging a wide range of members in developing the strategy and practices as a fresh opportunity to envision the future of the church and align priorities accordingly.
- Directing all church staff and lay leaders to be accountable to support the church's comprehensive strategy.
- Developing an annual plan that supports the church's strategy and that involves people in balanced and properly sequenced groups and events.
- Providing the best possible financial support to implement the strategy.
- Implementing the plan through specific monthly and weekly actions.

We will commit to a strategy that includes open groups by:

- Developing an annual plan that supports the church's thrust to lead people to faith in the Lord Jesus Christ and to build Great Commission Christians.
- Including as key elements of the plan ongoing and short-term Bible study groups and additional Bible study events, such as Vacation Bible School, that focus on foundational evangelism and foundational discipleship.
- Providing opportunities that create and foster fellowship and encouragement in the congregation.

We will commit to a strategy of corporate worship that transforms by:

- Enabling persons of all ages to respond to the presence, holiness, and revelation of Almighty God through prayer, praise, confession and repentance, confession of faith, Scripture reading and study, preaching, the ordinances, and offerings.

- Providing intentional and significant opportunities for corporate prayer calling upon God to direct the church.
- Creating an environment for worship that causes lost persons to respond to God in repentance and faith through the moving of God's Spirit.
- Challenging members to respond to ministry through service and missions.

We will commit to a strategy that includes closed groups by:
- Developing a discipleship perspective that reflects an intentional and holistic approach to guide disciples to grow in spiritual maturity and to equip believers for ministry.
- Providing a spiritually-sensitive environment that encourages believers to respond to Jesus' call to follow Him.
- Challenging believers to fulfill their call in the body of Christ.
- Developing believers' skills for service and missions.

We will commit to a strategy that includes ministry teams by:
- Creating an environment of prayer and urgency for people in need of God's love.
- Providing opportunities for people to participate regularly in ministry actions.
- Viewing ministry as an entry point for unbelievers.

2. Organize with Purpose
Our open groups will accomplish the objectives of leading people to faith in the Lord Jesus Christ and developing Great Commission Christians by:
- Using the concept of age-graded, Bible study groups as the primary organizing principle for these groups.
- Providing for all ages and generations including preschool, children, youth, young adults, and adults.
- Organizing the groups to provide key leaders responsible for engaging all persons to participate in the functions of the church.
- Relying on sound, learner-leader ratios proven to be effective for each age group in developing the age-group organizational structures.

Our closed groups will accomplish the objectives of equipping believers for ministry and building kingdom leaders by:

- Recognizing that God provides the believer a new identity in Christ and that transformation continues throughout each believer's lifelong relationship with Christ.
- Providing age-group ministries for preschool, children, youth, young adults, and adults.
- Providing for all special-interest ministries such as collegiates, singles, seniors, men's, women's, marriage, family, prayer, life-support, health, and recreation.
- Providing the leadership training system for the entire church to develop new leaders and to challenge experienced leaders.

3. Build Kingdom Leaders

We will build kingdom leaders and a leadership team through a leadership development strategy as an expression of faithfulness to Christ, His church, and His mission mandate by:

- Praying for God to call out leaders to serve Him through this ministry.
- Relying on the Holy Spirit to empower the church to develop servant leaders who depend on His power.
- Implementing a leader enlistment approach that focuses on helping people respond to their personal call and giftedness from God rather than an approach that is primarily concerned with filling church or organizational positions.
- Enlisting leaders for all church ministries who themselves are committed to cultivating and multiplying new leaders.
- Devoting major attention to open-group leadership meetings that focus on the mission, on relationships, and on Bible study.
- Providing closed-group training for all training tracks to equip leaders for their work and to enhance the quality of their leadership.
- Calling out people who will give their lives to evangelizing the lost and who are willing to participate in on-

going evangelism training and multiplication of evangelism leaders.

4. Develop Soul-Winners

We will lead leaders and members to become soul-winners and witnesses for Christ in all life settings, including the home by:

- Teaching members to view being a practicing soul-winner as the role of every believer.
- Challenging members continually to be aware of the spiritually lost people they encounter daily.
- Focusing attention on the responsibility of leaders and members to lead people to faith in the Lord Jesus Christ.
- Training leaders and members how to share the gospel through an intentional, ongoing strategy.
- Providing regular opportunities for leaders and members to share the gospel.

5. Win the Lost

We will engage in evangelistic actions that result in winning the lost to Christ, as well as other actions that focus on the unchurched and reclaim the spiritually indifferent, by:

- Involving members in discovering individual and family prospects.
- Maintaining up-to-date master and working prospect files and implementing an ongoing approach for making evangelistic prospect visitation assignments to members.
- Providing regular, specific times for evangelistic, outreach, and ministry visitation.
- Committing believers to witness for Christ in all life settings, including the home.
- Enrolling people anytime, anywhere in ongoing Bible study and other short-term Bible study groups.
- Teaching evangelistically, including foundational teaching that becomes the basis for a later conversion as the Holy Spirit brings conviction of sin.
- Challenging unchurched and/or spiritually indifferent individuals and families to commit to living as followers of Jesus Christ.

6. Assimilate People

We will assimilate individuals and families into the life of the church and facilitate their growth as disciples of Christ by:

- Encouraging new believers to identify with Christ and His church through baptism and church membership.
- Enrolling people in ongoing Bible study groups where they will be shown interest, support, and care as they build meaningful relationships with others.
- Identifying believers' gifts for service.
- Expecting members to share their faith and intentionally engaging them in evangelism training.
- Emphasizing regular participation in systematic Bible study as the foundational step of discipleship.
- Providing an atmosphere for building relationships with one another in an environment of grace, acceptance, support, and encouragement.
- Encouraging all believers to strengthen their walk with Christ by participating in other discipleship opportunities.
- Developing a system for tracking individual and family participation in ongoing Bible study and in discipleship groups.
- Developing a system for tracking actions that serve as indicators of spiritual growth and personal spiritual vitality.
- Providing opportunities for new Christians, church members, and their families to discover how they fit into the life and ministry of the church.
- Planning opportunities for individuals and families to pray together and to work together toward fulfilling the Great Commission.
- Promoting systematic biblical giving and the stewardship of life as the norm for believers.

7. Partner with Families

We will partner with parents and families to build the home as the center of biblical guidance by:

- Equipping disciples to strengthen family relationships.
- Providing an appropriate open Bible study group for every member of the family, including those with special needs.

- Providing training and resources to help parents fulfill their responsibility as the primary Bible teachers and disciplers of their children.
- Developing family-oriented evangelistic and ministry strategies to help families reach other families for Christ and the church and to minister to their needs.
- Providing closed-group training and enrichment experiences to strengthen marriage relationships.
- Building a leadership team that believes in and models the essential partnership of home and church in Bible teaching.
- Providing Bible study and devotional materials that encourage and support family worship and Bible study in the home.
- Exploring the possibilities for intergenerational ministries that enable the different generations to interact with each other rather than being isolated from one another.

8. Teach to Transform

We will engage individuals and families in the biblical model of instruction that leads to a progressive change of worldview, values, attitudes, and behaviors by:

- Preparing faithfully for the open-group Bible teaching session, including personal spiritual preparation and participation in leadership meetings.
- Encountering God's Word in an open Bible study group, guiding learners toward spiritual transformation in daily living and family relationships.
- Centering the open-group transformational teaching-learning process around these Bible teaching elements: acknowledge authority, search the Truth, discover the Truth, personalize the Truth, struggle with the Truth, believe the Truth, and obey the Truth.
- Preparing open-group lesson plans to teach in a variety of ways including relational, musical, logical, natural, physical, reflective, visual, and verbal approaches.
- Equipping parents to be the primary Bible teachers in their homes.
- Choosing open-group Bible study curriculum materials that lead learners to explore the entire counsel of God during their life stages.

- Providing a variety of closed-group training tracks that build on the biblical foundations laid in the open groups.
- Providing closed groups that offer rich, in-depth Bible study for believers.
- Choosing closed-group curriculum that leads learners to aggressively pursue spiritual transformation that impacts their life and witness at every level including the kingdom of God, new identity in Christ, relationships in the home and family, the church, work and school, the world (society and culture), and spiritual warfare (strongholds).
- Providing the best possible teaching resources that enable teachers to teach for spiritual transformation.
- Providing the best possible space and equipment as appropriate for age-group teaching and learning.

9. Mobilize for Ministry
We will take deliberate actions to meet the needs of individuals and families with compassion by:
- Remembering that the greatest need is to be in right relationship with the Lord.
- Challenging people to advance from the classroom to the market place.
- Helping identify ministry needs and informing leaders and members about ministry opportunities.
- Equipping individuals and families to minister to others in need in all settings.
- Determining the purpose of each ministry team.
- Mobilizing people to serve by moving them into ministry teams.
- Leading members and their families to be involved in ministry and missions projects.
- Involving the church family in supporting missionaries and mission work through prayer and giving.
- Encouraging Christians to influence secular culture, citizenship issues, and public policy with Christian principles.
- Creating an environment that encourages people to respond to God's call to Christian vocational ministry.
- Practicing apprenticeship and multiplication that leads

to new or expanded ministry and persons involved in ministry.

- Reporting the results toward accomplishing a specific ministry in the life of the church as a measure of accountability and sharing the fruit of the ministry to the church.

10. Multiply Leaders and Units

We will develop and implement an intentional process for continually multiplying leaders and new kingdom units by:

- Communicating the key relationship multiplication of leaders and units has to the overall mission of the church's strategy.
- Teaching every believer to be in service and on mission and to multiply themselves.
- Developing potential leader training ministry that helps members explore their leadership potential and possibilities.
- Making leader enlistment and multiplication of units an ongoing process rather than annual actions.
- Encouraging and supporting the initiative of existing Bible study groups to reproduce themselves through new Bible study groups that increase the opportunity to evangelize and disciple more people.
- Encouraging and supporting the efforts of leaders to identify prospective leaders and guide them toward service for Christ and His church.
- Starting new open groups, new closed groups, and new ministry teams.
- Engaging the church to start a new Vacation Bible School, a new Sunday School, or help to plant a new church mission.

Remember that our goal is to produce significant kingdom results over time. Our discussion of the ten essential actions that guide best church practice has taken us deep into the details of a comprehensive, churchwide process. We can now take a step back and look at the bigger picture — the relationship of the local church's growth to the kingdom.

Church Growth Not Isolated from the Kingdom

Total church growth parallels growth in God's kingdom. Healthy church growth will not occur in isolation from the kingdom, from the life and growth of other churches, or from what God is doing in the world. The ministry of a local church can never fulfill the Great Commission until it becomes a kingdom ministry. Only then will a church have the perspective, power, and vision it needs to grow as God intends.

Many churches' efforts are limited to one or two kingdom principles with little or no view of how much their efforts impact the world or the kingdom of God. Attention must be given to *all* kingdom principles if church growth is to occur.

> Healthy church growth will not occur in isolation from the kingdom.

Believers Are to Be Kingdom Citizens

God intends for His children to be world and kingdom citizens, fully committed to His purposes in the world.

A church is the most valuable resource God has in any community, state, or nation to minister to people. Government and social and humanitarian agencies cannot begin to match the power and resources the Lord can provide through His people who minister in His name.

We Must Commit Ourselves to Minister

We must commit ourselves to fellow believers and to others around us to minister to them in the power and authority of Christ. Churches cannot waste time, energy, effort, and resources doing things that are not a part of God's plan.

God's plan is basic: We are commissioned to go under the authority of Christ to evangelize the world, to baptize believers, and to disciple them in Christlikeness. Anything we choose to do in ministry that does not result in transforming people by God's grace and equipping them to minister with spiritual gifts is not a priority. Churches and believers who are led of the Lord to practice kingdom principles are those who discover the ministries that God intends for them.

> Anything we choose to do in ministry that does not result in transforming people by God's grace and equipping them to minister with spiritual gifts is not a priority.

EVERY PERSON IS A POTENTIAL MINISTER

You may be wondering: *Where am I going to get the leaders I need to implement the five essential functions?* Every unsaved person is a potential convert to be won and baptized. He or she also is a potential minister of God. The Lord seeks to save the lost and to impart His Spirit to them to be His ministers of reconciliation wherever He chooses to send them. This is the primary goal and function of every believer and local church. To do anything else is to depart from the gospel and the Great Commission. We are never to sacrifice the best things for good things.

WHERE DO WE GO FROM HERE?

Knowing where to go is not always easy, but it is easier than getting there. To have a basic understanding of the Great Commission, God's kingdom, the church, the essential kingdom functions of a local church, the results that follow those functions, and how to put those kingdom principles into practice is one thing. To change the direction of a church and to stop spending time and effort on good things while the best go untouched is quite another.

How can we change the life and culture of our churches to conform to God's will and work and to join Him on His mission to redeem our world? The answer can be summed up in one statement:

THE 1•5•4 PRINCIPLE

THE 1•5•4 PRINCIPLE

1 – Great Commission

5 – Functions
- Evangelism
- Discipleship
- Fellowship
- Ministry
- Worship

4 – Results
- Numerical Growth
- Spiritual Transformation
- Ministry Expansion
- Kingdom Advance

WHERE DO WE GO FROM HERE?

Throughout this book, I have avoided giving you methods to help you use God's kingdom principles for church growth. I have done this for three reasons:

First, methods are important and helpful, but a wide variety of methods can be used to employ these principles. Far too many methods exist to be dealt with in the scope of this book. In fact, my hope and prayer is that you will take these principles and develop your own methods to grow your church in your place. Be sure, though, that LifeWay Christian Resources stands ready with every available resource to assist you in growing your church.

Second, methods change, but these principles are permanent. They do not change.

Third, you need to become thoroughly familiar with these basic biblical principles before deciding on methods. You also need to know how these principles can work for you and your church. Then you need to know how you can use them to see your church begin to grow and develop as soon as possible.

Do these principles work? Absolutely. If they did not work, why would the Lord give them? I have used these principles in five different churches, and they worked every time. Each church was different and was located in a different part of the nation. One church was rural; one was in a transitional community; two were suburban; and one was in a small city. Each church was different in size of membership, and each had its own personality and circumstances. We employed the five kingdom functions in each church and saw the four results presented in this book produced in each one.

Because the churches were different, we sometimes used different methods and had different responses. While we had the four results, the sequence sometimes was different. In some cases we had large numerical increases quickly. In other cases we saw ministry and kingdom advance develop before we had significant numerical growth. In one church the spiritual growth of our members was the largest growth of the four areas. Later, under another pastor, the church began to grow numerically. In every case, however, the Lord gave growth in each of the four areas over a period of time.

I have not discovered any shortcuts to church growth. Growth is challenging, time-consuming work that demands our best. The results in changed lives make it worth every hour and every drop of perspiration expended.

Some churches grow numerically more quickly than others. Some churches mature spiritually for a time before many persons are added to the membership. Growth occurs as the Lord lives His life through individual believers and the congregation as a whole.

How can you apply the 1·5·4 kingdom principles of church growth in your church? Church growth begins where all things begin in the Christian life—in a right relationship with God. Every practical approach to applying these principles is based on our personal relationship with Him.

God speaks to His children in a variety of ways. We get our directions from Him about what He wants us to do in our communities and churches to reach people for Christ. He speaks to us through the Holy Spirit, through prayer, through His Word, through the fellowship of the church, and through human circumstances. Church growth is God's work, and we can do effective work for Him only when our relationship with Him is right.

Jesus said that His work was the work of Him who sent Him (John 9:4). He said to His disciples, "My food is to do the will of Him who sent Me and to finish His work" (John 4:34).

If Christ had a clear understanding that His task was to do the Father's work, we can do no less. We must seek the Father's presence and do His will. Paul reminds us that God "is working among you both the willing and the working for His good purpose" (Phil. 2:13).

The Lord speaks to us in a variety of ways, but He never will contradict His Word and His nature. Neither will God contradict Himself in what He tells different persons. He will not tell a layperson one thing and the pastor another. The Lord may not tell us everything we want to know, but He never will give contradictory directions to the church.

Corporate Prayer

Corporate prayer is the church in relationship with the Father, hearing from Him, and discerning His will and purpose for the church. Prayer opens the church to God's will and direction. God may wait for the church to pray before He releases His power to save those we care for and seek to reach. Church growth begins with a strategy of prayer. I have never known of a church growth method that did not involve prayer. Prayer is foundational to the Christian life. It is the heartbeat of vibrant Christians. Through prayer we talk to and hear from the Father. I do not know of any growing churches that do not pray fervently.

If you want your church to grow, pray for growth. An older pastor advised me about a decision in our church. He said: "Get before the Lord for about two weeks in prayer. When you get your answer, stay before Him for two more weeks to thank Him." The Lord promised:

"Ask of Me, and I will surely give the nations as Thine inheritance" (Ps. 2:8, NASB).

"Call to Me, and I will answer you, and I will tell you great and mighty things, which you do not know" (Jer. 33:3, NASB.)

"If you remain in Me and My words remain in you, ask whatever you want and it will be done for you" (John 15:7).

"You did not choose Me, but I chose you. I appointed you that you should go out and produce fruit, and that your fruit should remain, so that whatever you ask the Father in My name, He will give you" (John 15:16).

An effective prayer strategy begins when we pray, believing God will give us what He intends us to have. He has chosen to accomplish His work in this world through the prayers of His people.

Prayer takes us into places of spiritual warfare where God breaks the power of Satan and evil over persons' lives. Those in spiritual bondage will not be released through government programs and education. They can be rescued only by the power of God. We must pray that His power will release them from sin, satanic oppression, and separation from God.

If a church is to grow, the members must pray for God's will and power to be manifest, for persons to be saved, and for kingdom growth to occur in the church.

Intercessory prayer may be the most difficult ministry in the church, because nothing is more effective in winning the struggle with Satan than prayer. If your church is to grow, you and your people must pray.

LEADERSHIP

Effective Christian leadership is a crucial sector in church growth. Church leadership can be defined as leading the church to accomplish the Great Commission and bringing every believer for whom the leader is accountable to complete maturity in Christ. Leaders are called by God to follow Christ in a life of discipleship, using their spiritual gifts productively.

Kingdom Principles for Church Growth

The Holy Spirit

Another crucial factor in church growth is understanding and experiencing the Holy Spirit's ministry. Jesus' greatest teaching about the Holy Spirit is found in three chapters of the Gospel of John. Christ assured the disciples that although He must return to the Father following His death and resurrection, the Holy Spirit would come to them. The Spirit is the other "Counselor" (14:16-17) who would be with them forever. He is the "Spirit of truth." He also would have the responsibility of teaching them all things and recalling all things to their minds (14:26). He would not let the disciples forget Christ's words and would give them clear understanding of what Jesus meant long after He had returned to the Father.

The ministry of the Holy Spirit is absolutely essential to church growth. He came to bear witness of Christ in a hostile world (15:26-27). He came to convict the world of sin, its need for righteousness, and God's judgment (16:7-11). He also came to guide Jesus' followers into all truth and to show them things to come (16:13).

The Spirit's work in the first century is His work in every century. Without the Spirit, the church is powerless. Without Him, believers do not know and understand what God is doing in the world and what He wants them to do. Jesus sent the Spirit to help us in our work of reaching persons for salvation and growing them in the Christian life. He leads and guides us while He works in the lives of those who are lost, convicting them of their need for salvation. We cannot fulfill the Great Commission without the Spirit's wisdom and power.

The Holy Spirit also gives us fresh communications from the Father. Jesus said, "He will not speak on His own, but He will speak whatever he hears" (16:13). The Spirit's role is to communicate God's will, directions, and encouragement to us.

The Holy Spirit is our resource and power to do the work the Father gives us. Lost persons cannot be saved, believers cannot grow, and the church cannot be guided without the Holy Spirit's indwelling presence. We must learn to hear from the Spirit. We must yield ourselves to Him before we make decisions about strategies, plans, and resources in church growth.

The Bible

The surest, most consistent way the Lord speaks to us is through His Word. The Word is fresh each day because the Lord speaks through it daily. It is sure because it is truth without any mixture of error. A church and its people must make a commitment to study the Bible and live according to its truth.

We have no lack of Bible study. Bible study groups are everywhere. The issue is not so much how much we study the Bible. The issue is whether or not we hear the Lord speaking to us from the Bible and whether or not we are doing what He says in His Word.

Where Do We Go From Here?

People who question the nature and validity of the Bible as God's Word have little reason to live by what it says. The Bible's nature is in keeping with God's nature. God is the Author of the Bible; He is truth and does not lie. His Word is truth without error. God has given us His Word as a written guide for our lives. He speaks to us through His Word and wants us to do as He says.

Bible study and worship are cornerstones of any church. We must be careful, however, not to come to Bible study just for information. We are to come to Bible study to hear God speak to us through His Word in order to transform our lives, give us guidance and understanding in living, and to reveal Himself to us. Hebrews 4:12 declares:

"For the word of God is living and effective and sharper than any two-edged sword, penetrating as far as to divide soul, spirit, joints, and marrow; it is a judge of the ideas and thoughts of the heart."

If our churches are to grow, we must come to God's Word to hear from Him and to follow His will and way for our lives. Church growth strategies must include getting people into His Word—privately, in small groups, and in our worship services. Growing churches make God's Word a priority in ministry and practice.

Planning for Growth

Church growth is something the Lord does. Only God saves persons and only God grows churches. He invites us to join Him in His work, and we must never forget this important truth. However, we do need to plan. Planning for growth does not indicate a lack of faith. It does just the opposite. Planning assumes that God is at work in and around us and wants us to become a part of what He is doing. Church growth planning is a way to apply the Great Commission to our churches. Planning can be done many ways. Some planning methods are better than others; some are outdated; and some will fit your church better than others. Planning is good when it is done correctly.

Here is a planning process that will help you implement the Great Commission in the life and ministry of your church. Following the steps in this process will help you avoid some serious pitfalls along the way.

Commitment.—Planning for church growth begins with personal and church commitment to fulfill the Great Commission. We must come to the point where we are willing to do whatever the Lord asks and wants. We cannot determine what *we* want *our* church to be. We do not own our church; it is the Lord's to do with as He chooses. We are not to limit Him to the methods we know or think will work in our situation. Neither should we assume that the methods God uses in other churches are the same ones He will use in our church.

KINGDOM PRINCIPLES FOR CHURCH GROWTH

Commitment begins with an honest evaluation of our lives and churches. The best way to determine our direction is to see what the Lord is doing in our lives and churches at present. Is He using you and your church to reach the lost? Is He using you and your people to minister to the needs of individuals inside and outside your church? Are you discipling believers and equipping them for ministry? If Christ is not living His life through you and your church, something is wrong. Jesus made this wonderful promise to us in John 14:12:

"I assure you: The one who believes in Me will also do the works that I do. And he will do even greater works than these, because I am going to the Father."

I must ask myself when I examine my commitment to Christ, Am I consistently doing His works? If I am not or if my church is not, something is wrong.

The works Jesus did on earth revealed God. Everything He did pointed people to the Father. His miracles were signs that the kingdom had come and individuals could enjoy personal fellowship with the Father. He exorcised demons, healed the sick, and ministered to those who were frightened, hungry, and thirsty.

Our planning for church growth must include doing the works of the Father in our lives and in our local churches. The methods we choose must be consistent with kingdom principles of growth outlined in God's Word. If our plans do not include methods that fulfill the Great Commission, our success will be limited. If our methods do not result in the four dimensions of church growth, we need to change them. We need to spend much time with the Lord as we plan to use the methods He chooses.

Strategic planning for effective ministry.—Strategic planning is envisioning the future and allocating resources and effort to reach that vision. Each church needs to develop its own clearly defined growth strategy and its process for establishing its strategic priorities. Such a strategy will enlarge the church's vision of its growth potential. It also will protect the church from hindrances to growth and will give it the tools needed to realize its potential. The pastor and the church must see strategic planning as a process, not as a method or programmatic approach to planning.

Through a strategic mapping process, the pastor and other church leaders can develop the church's strategic priorities, based on the essential kingdom principles outlined in this book. This mapping process involves four steps. Let's briefly look at each step.

Step one focuses on gaining a strategic view of the church's work. This view includes a clear focus on the kingdom principles involved in church growth, the Great Commission, and the church members' spiritual giftedness. This step helps the church focus on its strengths in preparation for ministry.

Where Do We Go From Here?

Step two concentrates on establishing the church's strategic priorities. This step guides the church in determining which areas of its work will receive top priority. This section of the map is the heart of the strategic planning process.

Step three focuses on the actions the church will take as a result of the priorities it establishes. This step involves determining actions to be taken in open groups, corporate worship, closed groups, and ministry teams that are based on the five functions of the church, listed on pages 6 and 9 and treated in detail in chapter 3 of this book.

Step four enables the church to evaluate its progress toward its strategic priority goals.

Before a church designs its budget or establishes its calendar of events, church leaders should complete the strategic planning process. Completing this work before planning major actions and events will ensure that the church focuses its available resources on carrying out the Great Commission.

In corporate life, leaders spend hours developing their companies' vision and resourcing employees to reach that vision. Churches need to do similar planning with one important exception. Churches' visions must come from the Lord. Church leaders need to spend time together with the Lord in prayer, Bible study, and sharing to receive His vision for their work.

We know that God's will for every believer and church is to fulfill the Great Commission. How that is to be done in your church is a decision you and your church leaders must make with God's help and guidance. A vision statement should be developed, written, discussed, adopted, and communicated throughout the church. A vision statement should state who you are, what you do, and why it is significant. It should state how you believe God would have you fulfill the Great Commission. Your vision statement might be something like this one I have used in the past:

Our church will fulfill the Great Commission by sharing the love of God in Christ with every person through evangelizing, discipling, fellowshiping, ministering, and worshiping.

A vision statement is not easy to write. It may be easier to spend time with the Lord to get a sense of what He wants than it is to translate that inner direction into words that clearly communicate the ideas to others.

After the vision statement is developed, goals, action plans, and resources can be determined to fulfill the vision. You need to develop these in proper sequence in order to avoid doing actions that have no relationship to the vision God has given your church.

KINGDOM PRINCIPLES FOR CHURCH GROWTH

I have written this book to encourage you to do some basic things before you begin to use a method of church growth. I know from experience (sometimes painful) that the things discussed in this book are important. I can say from my experience these kingdom principles are biblical and they work in local churches. My prayer is that you and your church will commit yourselves to fulfilling the Great Commission under God's leadership and by His grace and power.

CONCLUSION

From the first until the last page of this book, I have attempted, with the Holy Spirit's leadership, to outline the biblical process of church growth. Commitment to this process can bring joy and fulfillment to your Christian life. It can breathe new life and a fresh perspective into your church.

This is not a book of church growth methods. It seeks to direct you and undergird you on the journey of growth our Lord desires for His churches. This is a journey of applying kingdom principles and fulfilling the Great Commission.

This process opens the door for you and your church to work at what works, to focus on the best, to experience a new freedom in the Lord, and to be assured that when Monday morning comes you will have no question about what you and your church are to do.

The kingdom principles of church growth are not new. No doubt, you have thought to yourself as you read this book, *I know that, I believe that*. Indeed, you are right. These principles are as eternal as God Himself and as applicable in our age of sin, frustration, violence, anxiety, anger, selfishness, hunger, poverty, materialism, and greed as they were the day God gave them.

My prayer is that you and your church will launch forth in faith with the assurance of God's power and promise to redeem humanity through Jesus Christ our Lord.

"Now may the God of peace, who brought up from the dead our Lord Jesus — the great Shepherd of the sheep — with the blood of the everlasting covenant, equip you with all that is good to do His will, working in us what is pleasing in His sight, through Jesus Christ, to whom be glory forever and ever. Amen" (Heb. 13:20-21).

ADDENDUM: FAITH – AN EMERGING BEST PRACTICE

FAITH is the primary evangelism methodology recommended to the churches by LifeWay Church Resources as a comprehensive plan for training church members to become soul winners.

As envisioned, the FAITH Sunday School Evangelism Strategy® intersects with all four of the church practice strategies through open groups, corporate worship, closed groups, and ministry teams. Churches are calling out FAITH leaders in the context of corporate worship, integrating FAITH into the Sunday School or the open group experience, creating a fresh stream for building leaders and equipping disciples through the closed group, and viewing FAITH as part of a process to assimilate new believers into the life and ministry of the church.

FAITH can be viewed as an emerging, holistic church practice for keeping evangelism and discipleship together while building leaders and multiplying ministry. Approximately 6,845 churches and 28,540 individuals have been trained to date through 344 clinics and institutes. Qualitative church results suggest that the FAITH Sunday School Evangelism Strategy® is increasingly being viewed by participating churches as a holistic process to implement key church practice. More long-term quantitative results will be necessary to assess the strategic impact of FAITH on church practice.

While FAITH is activated as an evangelism strategy through the open group or Sunday School, ongoing training at the church level occurs in the closed group. The FAITH evangelism strategy requires a closed group approach for training leaders and members in the basic, advanced, and discipleship levels. A high level of commitment is expected by the pastor and Sunday School or open-group leaders.

FAITH — An Emerging Best Practice

FAITH Impact on Church Practices

Based on testimonies from churches using the FAITH evangelism strategy and anecdotal research, FAITH is having impact on participating churches in at least the following ways:

- Re-energizing pastors and congregations
- Providing a common focus for priorities in church ministry
- Increased visitation participation and consistency in personal ministry of Sunday School classes
- Increased Sunday School enrollment and attendance
- Increased worship attendance
- Increased baptisms
- Growing sense of purpose for Sunday School classes and departments
- Growing need for software support and applications related to FAITH participation, Sunday School, and general prospect discovery
- Deeper reliance on prayer

Key Components of FAITH

The Sunday School Class. — At the heart of FAITH is the Sunday School class. The FAITH strategy focuses on the work already assigned to the classes of each age division. Three-member FAITH Teams are enlisted from the same Sunday School class or department. Those Teams are assigned visits to prospects and members of their classes or departments. Class members not on Teams are praying and are hearing answers to their prayers. They are welcoming and encouraging new members.

Some visits will be to members who need caring or maintenance. Many members have short- or long-term crises or concerns, while other individuals have dropped out of ongoing participation. Other visits will be to individuals targeted for the class; these individuals do not know the Lord and/or are not participating in any ongoing Bible study. Who better to try to reach them than members with similar age, needs, and life situations? FAITH Teams nurture the people being visited for their own classes.

Weekly Sunday School Leadership Meetings. — Leaders of Sunday School meet regularly to focus on people issues as they are impacted by God's Word and the ministry of caring for believers. As prospects are discovered and visited and members are ministered to, follow-up actions are planned and implemented. These ongoing meetings focus on helping a class accomplish all of its functions rather than just preparation to teach God's Word, as important as that is. People meeting together to plan Bible study, outreach and evangelism, fellowship activities, and ministry efforts with people and their families in mind give these meetings intentionality, focus, and vitality. When Sunday School leaders meet weekly to prepare, the likelihood also increases that learners will encounter God's Word in a way that transforms them and enables them to continue living out their faith in daily relationships.

FAITH Group Leaders/Coordination. — Leaders who relate to multiple FAITH Teams, called FAITH Group Leaders, meet weekly to coordinate assignments, processes, and needed follow-up. When a church first begins FAITH, it may have only two or three Group Leaders. These leaders help build accountability and motivation into the FAITH ministry. Group Leaders are among FAITH's best and strongest promoters, especially as the strategy grows.

Sunday School Evangelism Training. — Integral to FAITH is an intentional process and plan to train laypeople to share their faith using a simple FAITH Visit Outline, which includes an easy-to-remember gospel presentation based on the word FAITH as an acrostic. Training includes classwork, home study, and on-the-job training.

Sixteen consecutive sessions of training, visitation, and home study provide enough information and practice for learners to see their trained Team Leader model how to make a visit. Sessions allow time to put into practice a recommended visit sequence and to learn the gospel presentation. A 16-week semester facilitates believers growing as Great Commission Christians. Over 16 weeks, trainees experience firsthand opportunities to learn the gospel presentation and to share it personally as they visit Sunday School members and prospects.

Not only do participants learn how to share the gospel, they also are trained in how to build bridges to people through Sunday School. They learn to share benefits of Sunday School in their Sunday School testimony. Learners make Sunday School ministry visits to members as well as evangelistic visits to prospects. They learn how to follow up through a caring small group. They learn how to build bridges of love through Sunday School.

For adults and students, the training plan and content for the first 16 sessions of FAITH are provided in *A Journey in FAITH: Facilitator Guide and Journal.* Subsequent 16-week courses — in FAITH Advanced and FAITH Discipleship — include similar resources.

Public Profession of a Personal Decision. — There is a big difference between leading a person to make a personal commitment to Christ and that person's deciding to make a public profession of faith. FAITH intentionally links persons through the nurturing ministry and ongoing fellowship of their Sunday School classes and helps them come to the point of making a public declaration of faith.

FAITH — An Emerging Best Practice

FAITH Advanced specifically trains Teams to return to someone who has made a profession of faith, to talk about baptism as a step of obedience.

Assimilation into the Life of the Church. — One reason many converts do not follow up on an earlier profession of faith is because church leaders have not helped them relate to the church and other Christians. When we build bridges that connect new converts to Sunday School, we increase the possibility of their being baptized, assimilated into the church, and discipled to follow Christ throughout their lives. FAITH intentionally helps build those bridges.

Discipleship of New Believers and of Those Who Are Being Trained. — A necessary part of assimilation is helping new believers grow in their faith. At the same time, an intentional distinctive of FAITH training is to help each participant grow in a personal journey of faith. Learners and Team Leaders model a process of experiencing and sharing how God is at work in their lives. While all courses have this goal, FAITH Discipleship courses emphasize this process.

Teams Trained to Equip Others. — Once a person is trained by a mentor in evangelism, he or she is prepared and energized to mentor a team of two other persons in the same process. Members trained in evangelism generally become more enthusiastic about being involved in other aspects of kingdom work. Sustained evangelism training captures the best of what Christ has empowered His people to do: obey the Great Commission and teach others to do so.

Much like the pieces of a puzzle, these components fit together, blend, and overlap. They are vital to Sunday School, and they are vital to the FAITH Sunday School Evangelism Strategy®. They fit together to create a coherent whole—a Sunday School ministry energized by people who are intentionally and strategically reaching out to and caring for people.

Strategic Assumptions About FAITH Training

- The FAITH Sunday School Evangelism Strategy® is a churchwide approach to evangelism training that is implemented through a church's Sunday School ministry. The strategy is designed to equip participants to become soul-winners.

- The pastor is the main leader and promoter of FAITH in his church. He consistently promotes FAITH and Sunday School ministry, models FAITH, and teaches FAITH.

- FAITH training is based on 16 consecutive sessions of training in evangelism, one session per week at a time other than Sunday morning. Each 16-week segment is called a semester.

KINGDOM PRINCIPLES FOR CHURCH GROWTH

- All participants are required to complete the first 16-week foundational semester (FAITH Basic, A Journey in FAITH) before moving to FAITH Advanced (Building Bridges Through FAITH) for the second 16-week semester, and then to subsequent FAITH Discipleship courses. Participants in FAITH Advanced and FAITH Discipleship are equipped to train others in FAITH.

- A 16-week semester of training requires a commitment by learners to participate in classroom study, on-the-job training, and home study.

- Participants include "Team Leaders" who have been trained and are equipped to lead a team in FAITH home visits and mentoring. Two new "Team Learners" who have committed to receive training further comprise a team.

- Each FAITH team is comprised of at least one person of each gender.

- Ideally, the team leader and learners are members of the same Sunday School class or department and are visiting prospects assigned to their class/department in order to integrate evangelism through Sunday School. Some visits will be for the purpose of class ministry contacts while others are for the purpose of taking a neighborhood opinion poll.

- Team learners are responsible for memorizing the entire FAITH Visit Outline. The FAITH Visit Outline takes approximately 30 minutes to complete when introductions are made, the gospel is presented, and an invitation is offered and important commitments are made by the person being visited. Learners participate in home visits, expanding their role each week to share in a visit those presentation elements studied in the classroom and at home.

- Team leaders are responsible for leading learners to put into practice the parts of the visit for which they have received training. Team leaders are responsible for leading "Team Time," when learners recite memorization from home study and previous sessions.

- The only people who can teach FAITH in a church are (1) those who have participated in a FAITH Training Clinic at a host church certified to teach FAITH and (2) individuals trained in the local church under the leadership of someone who has completed training in a clinic. All are encouraged to attend a clinic to gain a wider scope and understanding of the FAITH strategy.

At the conclusion of 16 weeks of the foundational semester of training (FAITH Basic, A Journey in FAITH), learners should be equipped to be soul-winners — fully capable and confident in conducting a FAITH visit, in presenting the gospel of Jesus Christ, and in sharing their faith in any life-witness opportunity. For more information, call toll-free 1-877-324-8498.